Ancestor Worship

VOLUME I:
A BRIEF HISTORY OF THE ALLEN, SABINE, DAVIS,
ADAMS AND DANA FAMILIES OF NEW ENGLAND

BARON COMSTOCK

Et misericordia eius a
progenie in progenies
Timentibus eum.

Ancestor Worship

Volume I: A Brief History of the Allen, Sabine, Davis, Adams and Dana Families of New England

Ancestor Worship Publishing
1315 S. Allec Street
Anaheim, CA 92805 U.S.A.
orders@ancestorworshippublishing.com;
http://www.ancestorworshippublishing.com

All rights reserved. No part of this book may be reproduced or transmitted in any form or by any means, electronic or mechanical, including photocopying, recording or by any information storage and retrieval system, without written permission from the author, except for the inclusion of brief quotations in a review.

Copyright ©2011 by Baron Comstock

Edition ISBN's
    Print version   978-0-9832021-0-3
    Electronic version   978-0-9832021-1-0

Front and back cover photo is of Armena (Allen) McLellan taken about 1866.

Volume I

The Ancestors of Ebenezer Allen
and
his wife, Mehetabel Dana

To
the children

at Comstock
St. Fidelis of Sigmaringen
2011

Contents

Introduction	ix
Preface	xix
Chapter 1 The Allens of Dedham and Medfield	1
Chapter 2 James and John Allen: The Founding Generation	13
Chapter 3 The Allen Family and the Sabine Family in Medfield and Rehoboth: The Second Generation	21
Chapter 4 The Daniel Allen Sr. Family in Pomfret and His Marriage to Hannah Davis: The Third Generation	31

Chapter 5   43
    Daniel Allen Jr. Marries Mary Adams:
    The Fourth Generation

Chapter 6   53
    The Marriage of Ebenezer Allen and Mehetabel Dana:
    The Fifth Generation

Bibliography   101

Name Index   103

Introduction

This is a history of my ancestors. Some twenty volumes are to follow, but in this first volume I begin with the ancestors of my great-great-grandmother Armena (Allen) McLellan's great-grandparents: Ebenezer Allen and his wife, Mehetabel Dana. Some of the families treated in subsequent volumes will be: the Putnam, Hall, Prescott, Bulkeley, Mott, Delano, Aldrich, Morehouse, McLellan and Winslow families.

Three pedigrees follow this introduction. The first traces the descent of Armena from Ebenezer and Mehetabel; the second traces Ebenezer's ancestors from their arrival in New England in the Great Puritan Migration to his birth in 1737. The third traces Mehetabel's ancestors in like manner to her birth in 1738.

The pedigree charts referred to in the text are located at the end of the volume.

Ancestor Worship

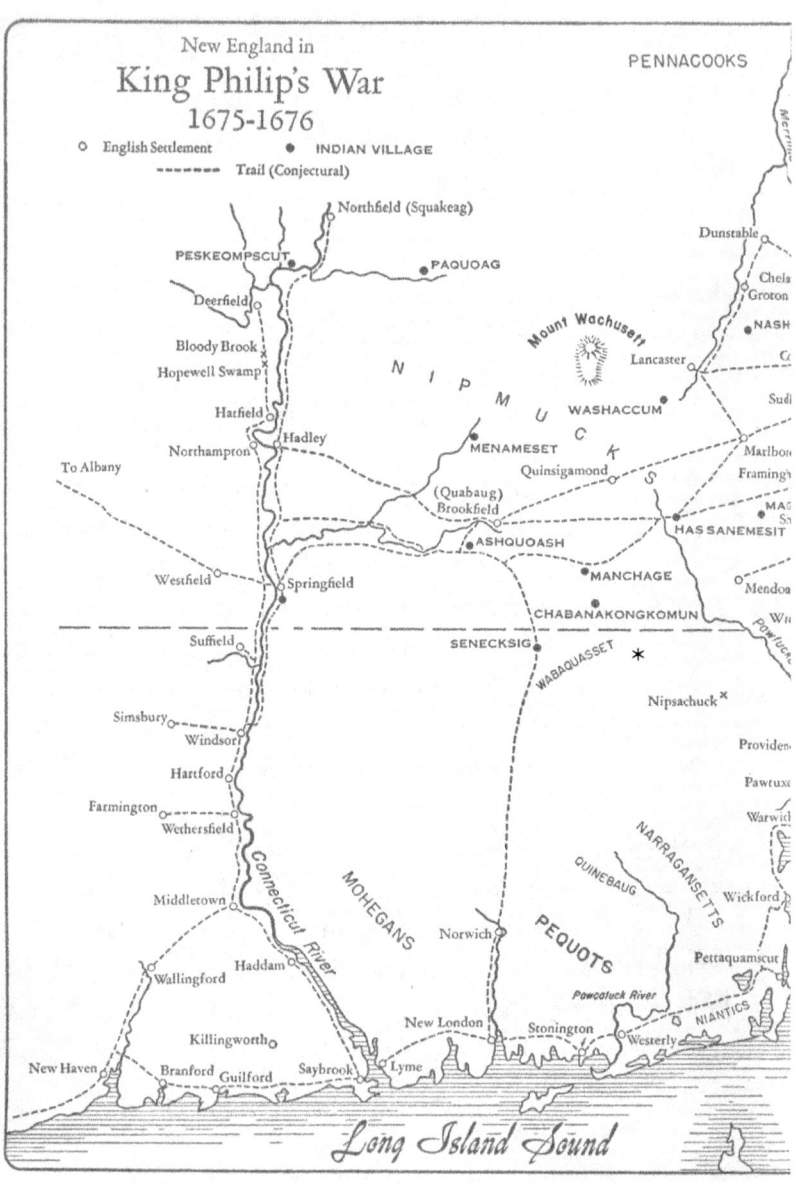

"Map New England in King Philip's War", from FLINTLOCK AND TOMAHAWK: New England in King Philip's War by Douglas E. Leach. Copyright ©1958 and renewed 1986 by Douglas Edward Leach. Used by permission of W.W. Norton & Company, Inc.

*Wabaquasset Indian Country, where the towns of Woodstock and Pomfret in Windham County, Connecticut were founded.

Introduction

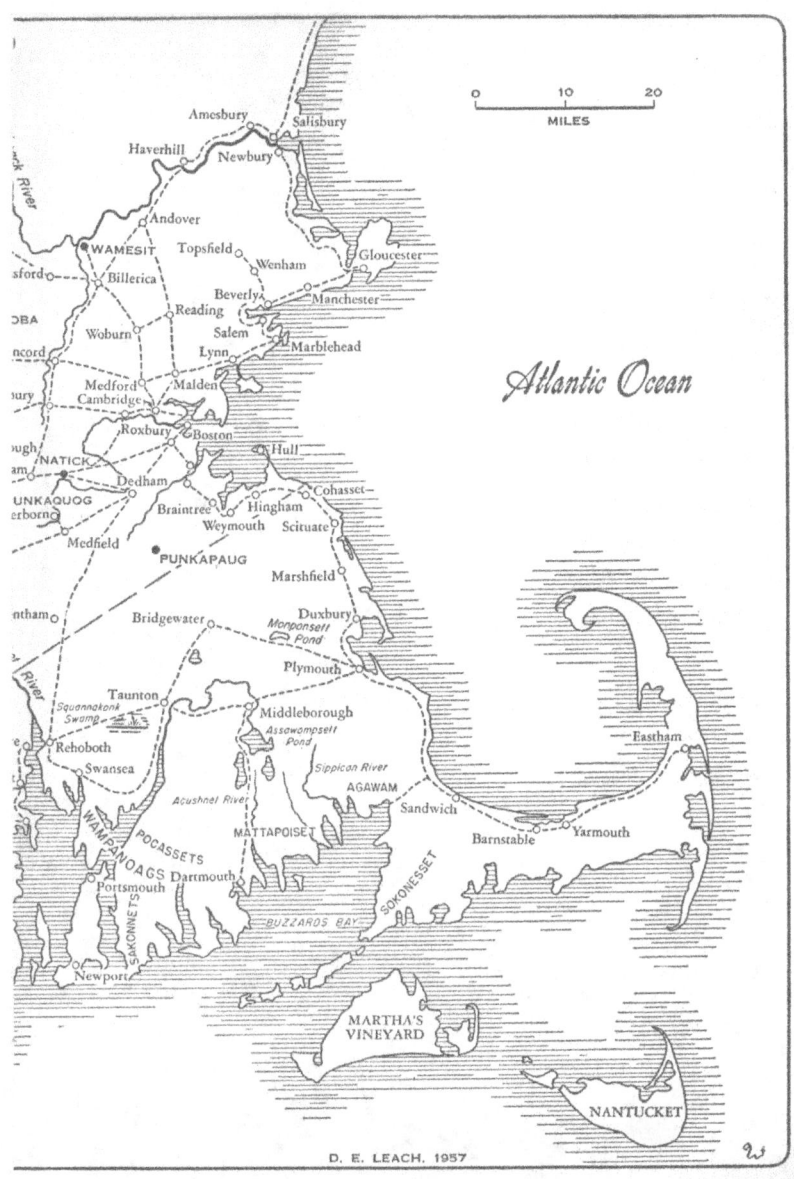

CHART A:
The descent of Armena Allen from Ebenezer Allen and his wife, Mehetabel Dana

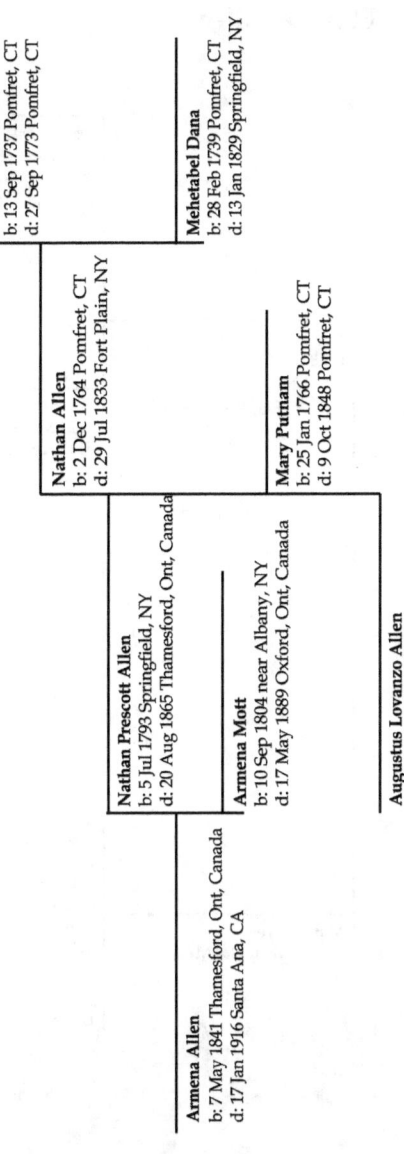

Ancestor Worship

CHART B:
The Ancestors of Ebenezer Allen

Daniel Allen Sr.
b: 21 Apr 1681 Medfield, MA
m: 11 Sep 1705 Woodstock, CT
d: 10 Apr 1759 Pomfret, CT

Daniel Allen Jr.
b: 28 Jul 1706 Pomfret, CT
m: 12 Nov 1728
d: 14 Apr 1776 Brooklyn, CT

Hannah Davis
b: 21 Mar 1680 Roxbury, MA
d: 17 Apr 1754 Pomfret, CT

Ebenezer Allen
b: 13 Sep 1737 Pomfret, CT
m: 10 Dec 1760 Pomfret, CT to Mehetabel Dana
d: 27 Sep 1773 Pomfret, CT

Joseph Adams
b: 25 Aug 1668 Medfield, MA
-sold land in Medfield in 1721 and moved with his family to Canterbury, CT
d: 9 Dec 1748 Canterbury, CT

Mary Adams
b: 1705 Medfield, MA
d: CT

Unknown

xiv

Introduction

- **Joseph Allen**
  b: 24 Jun 1654 Medfield, MA
  m: 10 Nov 1673
  d: 14 Jan 1703 Medfield, MA
  - **James Allen**
    b: England
    m: 1638 Dedham, MA
    d: 1676 Medfield, MA
  - **Anna Guild**
    d: 1673 Medfield, MA

- **Hannah Sabine**
  b: 22 Oct 1654 Rehoboth, MA
  d: 1729 Medfield, MA
  - **William Sabine**
    b: 11 Oct 1609
    d: 8 Jul 1686 Rehoboth, MA

- **Joseph Davis**
  b: 12 Oct 1647 Roxbury, MA
  m: 28 Oct 1670 Roxbury, MA
  d: 25 Dec 1717 Roxbury, MA
  - **William Davis**
    b: England
    d: 1683 Roxbury, MA

- **Sarah Chamberlain**
  b: 18 Dec 1649 Woburn, MA
  d: 25 Dec 1717 Roxbury, MA
  - **Edmund Chamberlain**
    b: 1617 England
    m: 1647 Roxbury, MA
    d: 1696 Woodstock, CT
  - **Mary Turner**
    b: 1625 Roxbury, MA
    d: 7 Dec 1669 Roxbury, MA

- **Peter Adams**
  b: 1 Mar 1622 Kings Weston, Eng
  d: 23 Oct 1690 Medfield, MA
  - **Henry Adams**
    b: 12 Jan 1582 Barton St. David, England
    m: 1609
    d: Oct 1646 Braintree, MA
  - **Edith Squire**
    b: 29 May 1587 Charlton Mackrell, England
    d: 21 Jan 1673 Medfield, MA

- **Rachel Newcomb**
  b: 13 Nov 1631 Braintree, MA
  d: 23 Oct 1690 Medfield, MA
  - **Francis Newcomb**
    b: 1605 Sudbury, England
    d: 27 May 1692 Braintree, MA
  - **Rachel Brackett**
    b: 28 Apr 1614 Sudbury, England
    d: 5 Jan 1685 Braintree, MA

Ancestor Worship

CHART C:
The Ancestors of Mehetabel Dana

Daniel Dana
b: 20 Mar 1663 Cambridge, MA
m: about 1691
d: 10 Oct 1749 Cambridge, MA

Ebenezer Dana
b: 12 Dec 1711 Cambridge, MA
m: 16 Nov 1728 Pomfret, CT
d: 19 Aug 1762 Havana, Cuba

Naomi Croswell
b: 5 Dec 1670 Charlestown, MA
d: 24 Feb 1751 Cambridge, MA

Mehetabel Dana
b: 28 Feb 1739 Pomfret, CT
m: 10 Dec 1760 Pomfret, CT
d: 13 Jan 1829 Springfield, NY

Thomas Goodell
b: 30 Oct 1676 Salem, MA
m: 2 Dec 1698 Beverly, MA
d: 22 Oct 1766 Pomfret, CT

Mehetabel Goodell
b: 16 Mar 1717 Pomfret, CT
d: 24 Oct 1794 Pomfret, CT

Sarah Horrell
b: 1 Jun 1684
d: 5 Nov 1750 Pomfret, CT

Introduction

Richard Dana
b: 31 Oct 1617 Manchester, England
m: about 1648
d: 2 Apr 1690 Cambridge, MA

Ann Bullard
b: 1626 England
d: 15 Jul 1711 Cambridge, MA

Robert Bullard
b: 1598 Barnham, England
d: 24 Apr 1639 Watertown, MA

Ann
b: 1604 Barnham, England
d: 1626 Watertown, MA

Thomas Croswell
b: 1633 England
d: 30 Aug 1708 Charlestown, MA

Priscilla Upham
b: about 1642 Weymouth, MA
d: 8 Dec 1717 Charlestown, MA

Deacon John Upham
b: about 1597 Bicton, England
m: at Bicton, England
d: 25 Feb 1681 Malden, MA

Elizabeth Slade
b: 1603 Bicton, England
d: 2 Dec 1670 Malden, MA

Zachariah Goodell
b: 31 May 1640 Salem, MA
m: 30 Apr 1666 Salem, MA
d: 30 Jun 1715 Salem, MA

Robert Goodale
b: 16 Aug 1601 Dennington, England
d: 12 Oct 1682 Salem, MA

Catherine Killiam
b: 16 Mar 1606 Dennington, England
d: 10 Sep 1666 Salem, MA

Elizabeth Beauchamp
b: 23 Jul 1648 Salem, MA
d: 31 Dec 1666 Salem, MA

Edward Beauchamp
b: 1612 Southwark, England
d: 29 Mar 1668 Salem, MA

Mary

Humphrey Horrell, Jr.
b: about 1650 Maine
d: 9 Feb 1710 Beverly, MA

Humphrey Horrell Sr.
b: about 1605 England
d: 1683 Beverly, MA

Unknown

Sarah Unknown
b: 1652 Beverly, MA
d: 1687 Beverly, MA

Baron Comstock with his great-Aunt Charlotte Gertrude (on right) and her mother's stepsister, Blanche Bishop on the Eastlake Divan

Preface

Seated upon her grandmother, Armena (Allen) McLellan's Eastlake rocker, my great-aunt Charlotte Gertrude reminisced about California before the automobile: her family's horse and buggy trips to Laguna Beach where the ladies collected mussels in their skirts; an excursion with horses and wagons to Yosemite where the Flora Dora Girls were staying at the lodge; and the horse-drawn tram passing up and down Figueroa Boulevard in Los Angeles.

The house of my great aunt's father stood on Figueroa Boulevard, opposite the University of Southern California. She would ride the horse-drawn tram to her school—Cumnock Academy for Girls, where the buildings evoked Stratford-upon-Avon; or uptown for a matinee at the Orpheum starring Ethel Barrymore in *The Twelve Pound Look*.

On Figueroa, Senator Reginaldo del Valle's family were my great-aunt's neighbors, and she would sometimes see the Senator doze off on the tram and miss his stop. The del Valle's retained a part of their Mexican land grant, Rancho Camulos, the inspiration for the popular novel, *Ramona,* and the Senator's daughter,

Lucretia, appeared in the play based upon this novel. To celebrate her stage debut, Lucretia and my great-aunt (students together at Cumnock) went to the Hotel Alexandria (abode of the silent movie idol, Valentino) to the Tea Room, and there, for the first time, saw women smoking in public.

My great-aunt's father, Nathan John Frederick McLellan, instructed his children to address him as "Fred" hoping to provoke fuddy-duddies. He owned "McLellan's Horse Market" on Main Street in Los Angeles and kept Trotting horses to race at Agricultural Park—a park replaced long ago by the Los Angeles Coliseum in the stable behind his house on Figueroa.

In the days to come, Fred's father, John McLellan (who owned a dry goods store in Santa Ana and sent his daughter, Minnie, to the University of Southern California), would predict that the automobile would ruin the county; but Fred would go on to buy a bright purple Mitchell automobile with red leather upholstery. He bought his youngest son, my grandfather, his first pair of long pants to wear when he drove the Mitchell.

My great-aunt was press secretary for the University Book Club and read Schopenhauer with the Book Club's ladies. Ladies clubs and Schopenhauer led to women's suffrage, and Fred would accompany my great-aunt to the polling place, though her mother, Lillie, preferred to stay at home. Lucretia del Valle married America's Ambassador to the Shah of Persia, and went off to improve the lot of women there.

In America, an economic disturbance left Fred in reduced circumstances. He salvaged from the wreck of his fortune a turkey farm in the bleak hinterlands of Kern County. Becoming a booker of oil leases, his fortunes were revived and he returned with his wife and daughter to the suburbs of Los Angeles where he lived out his days in the foothills of the San Gabriel Mountains.

There, in 1948, in a town named Monrovia, at the age of seventy-three, Fred died. It was the very year, and the very town, in which I, Baron Comstock, was born.

In 1964, sixteen years after Fred's death, his daughter, my great-aunt, Charlotte Gertrude, age seventy-one, was in her little parlor in Monrovia sitting upon her grandmother's platform rocker and reminiscing about California before the automobile.

In her little parlor, there were three rocking chairs, an Eastlake bookcase and an Eastlake divan—all furniture that had belonged to her grandparents, John and Armena (Allen) McLellan. The parlor's walls were decorated with oil paintings, charcoal sketches and watercolors—the works of artistic ancestresses. One landscape depicted the great sycamores on Uncle Prescott Allen's Ranch near Santa Ana. An oil painting commemorated Aunt Johanna (Allen) Mitchell with a still life featuring her Bible, a snuffed candle, and a wilted rose. But among all these relics, the Eastlake bookcase loomed talismanicly. Bronze medallions of a "Cavalier" and "Lady" embellished its locked doors. A bewildering concoction of elaborate moldings, colored glass, fretted hardware and inlaid burl wood, a pedestal atop its cornice was surmounted by Armena's sewing box fashioned to resemble a Greek goddess's rose-water vessel.

How far away the world of sewing boxes and trotting horses and Eastlake bookcases! A world as lost as the world of "Cavaliers" and "Ladies"; as lost as the world of Robin Hood and Maid Marion! Yet in my great-aunt's little parlor, amid the watercolors and rocking chairs, a key to that far off world seemed…

…and in fact, in that year, 1964, my great-aunt was holding, in her beautiful diamond-bespangled hand, a key—a small skeleton key. And she was walking to the Eastlake bookcase—unlocking its glass doors—opening its doors and revealing, inside, the collected books of John and Armena (Allen) McLellan. Bound in yellow calf were Josephus' *Jewish War*, a *Life of President Garfield*, Greeley's *American Conflict*, and a *Complete Shakespeare*. Two large quarto volumes of Longfellow's poetry were bound in brown morocco. *Brandt's Poems* and *Pilgrim's Progress* were in embossed and padded leather. *Uncle Tom's Cabin*, Stanley's *Adventures in Africa*, Ramona and President Grant's *Travels* were bound in ornate polychrome cloth boards. Large quarto editions of *Paradise Lost* and *The Inferno* were illustrated by Gustave Doré. And scattered among these were Crofut's *Overland Railroad Guide*—used by John and Armena to plot their travels from America's East to America's West; a *History of the Methodist Episcopal Church in Canada*; a *New York City Public School Directory* in which Armena's uncle Horatio Philanzo Allen is listed as a board member; and *The Vicar of Wakefield* inscribed to Armena in 1857 as a Sunday School prize "for good behavior, regular attendance and diligence in study."

...Yet it was for none of these that my great-aunt had opened the bookcase. Extracting from it a slim unprepossessing volume with a faux morocco spine, and giving it to me, I read on its yellow cover a title much embellished with Eastlake ornaments:

*A Brief History
of the
Allen, Putnam, Hall,
Grosvenor
and Other Families*

Preface

This slim volume was a genealogical treatise published in 1895 and written, in his old age, by Armena's Uncle Augustus Lovanzo Allen (twin brother of Horatio Philanzo). All those years ago it was intended by my great aunt to assist me with a high school history assignment, but it serves me here as the foundation upon which this volume (written in my old age) is based.

Where Augustus has made a mistake in his volume, where he is flagrantly fanciful or culpably ignorant of known facts, I correct him. But my correction, I hope, is always administered with the humility a disciple owes his master. For it was my great-great-great-great Uncle Augustus who first ventured forth into the near impenetrable jungle foliage of our family trees, and our adventure lies in following him.

I must have read Uncle Augustus' book with some care after my great-aunt gave it to me, since I can remember regaling rapt auditors, three years later, as a college freshman—with its delineation of my descent from Rev. Peter Bulkeley, founder of Concord, Massachusetts.

This Bulkeley descent brightened the gloom during my dreary years at the University of Southern California. I spent more and more time on genealogical researches. I discovered that Rev. Peter Bulkeley was descended from William Longsword, Earl of Salsbury, who's son was killed on crusade with Saint Louis. I discovered that William Longsword was the bastard son of King Henry II, who was in turn descended from St. Margaret of Scotland, St. Olav of Norway and the Devil. I discovered that St. Olav was descended from the Norse Gods. So that when at last the University issued its edict expelling me from its precincts, I received the sentence with the equanimity of one accustomed to suffering the envy of mortals *sub specie aeternitatis*. As the descendent of Royal Christian Saints, Norse

Gods and the Devil, my equanimity was imperturbable, and, indeed, remained unperturbed for some forty years, until, in 2004, *The New York Times* reported that both ridiculous candidates for the Presidency of the United States were claiming to be descended from Rev. Peter Bulkeley.

But now, if I am to record the history of all my ancestors (beginning with the Allens), I must hurry, for like Uncle Augustus who was eighty-six when he published his *Brief History*, I too am old.

Preface

Miss E. Kathleen Ross reads Longfellow's *Death of the Poet* before the Eastlake bookcase in the Eastlake Rocker.

CHAPTER 1

THE ALLENS OF DEDHAM AND MEDFIELD

A RMENA ALLEN WAS BORN IN 1841. Two hundred and four years before her birth, in 1637, her ancestor, James Allen, sailed from Old England to New England. From James Allen to Armena Allen, the Allen family pedigree comprises eight generations; and Armena's Uncle Augustus, in his *Brief History of the Allen Family*, relates what he knew—or thought he knew—about those generations. More is known today.

When James Allen arrived in the Massachusetts Bay Colony, the English had already settled several towns there. Traveling from Boston Back Bay up the Charles River, James would have passed both Newtown (renamed "Cambridge" the next year) and Watertown—towns settled by Puritans who had arrived with Winthrop's fleet in 1630. By 1635, Watertown was overcrowded and had petitioned Massachusetts General Court for land farther up the Charles. Dedham Township was granted to the petitioners in 1636—two hundred square miles on the Charles' left bank. James Allen was among Dedham's first settlers. He was the "cousin" (a word apt to mean "nephew" in the seventeenth century) of the Reverend John Allen, Dedham's first minister.

In 1651, fifteen years after Dedham's founding, two new towns were established within its original township borders: Natick, a town for Christian Indians; and Medfield, a town farther up the Charles for pioneers from Dedham. Medfield was the forty-third town incorporated in the Massachusetts Bay Colony, and James Allen was one of its first thirteen proprietors.

Medfield's name may have been derived from "Metfield" in Suffolk, England—a village near the villages of Wrentham and Fressingham from which many of Dedham's early settlers came. The Rev. John Allen, before his emigration, had been curate in Wrentham, Suffolk, and another new town within Dedham Township's borders would later be called Wrentham.

In 1638, in Dedham, James Allen married Anna Guild, and their first six children were born there. In 1652, the year after their move to Medfield, their seventh and last child, Joseph Allen, was born. Armena (Allen) McLellan was a descendant of Joseph Allen, the son of James, through a son of Joseph named Daniel who left Medfield for Connecticut Colony. But before setting out for Connecticut in pursuit of Armena's ancestors, let us take a brief look at some of the Allens who remained in Medfield.

In 1673, twenty-one years after his birth, Joseph Allen married Hannah Sabin, and, in the same year, was granted land in Medfield on the Natick Road near Castle Hill. The land granted to Joseph remained in the Allen family for two hundred and eighty-seven years—for seven generations—and became known as the Allen Place. It was sold out of the family by Miss Lucy Allen in 1936.

The children of Joseph and Hannah (Sabin) Allen were Joseph Jr., Hannah, Daniel, David, Noah, Eleazer, Jeremiah,

Hezekiah, Abigail, and Nehemiah—good puritan names chosen from the Old Testament.

Joseph Allen died in Medfield at the Allen Place in 1703, but his will was not probated until his youngest son, Nehemiah, came of age in 1720. It was then that Joseph's son, Noah, succeeded to the Allen Place. Since the Allen Place provided for the family of only one son, Joseph provided land for his other sons elsewhere. Armena's ancestor, Noah's brother, Daniel,[1] had been provided with land in Pomfret Township, Connecticut and there on June 2, 1735, he signed a declaration that he had "received of my brother, Noah Allen of Medfield, the sum of six pounds in bills of credit" and "do quit and discharge the estate of my honored father, Joseph Allen…"

In Medfield, Noah would become hopelessly, if harmlessly, insane; and his care, together with the care of the Allen Place and seven children, fell upon his wife, Sarah Gay. Sarah lived to be ninety—seeing her son, Noah Jr., take her husband's place in the Allen Place. Noah Jr. was a selectman in Medfield in 1766—the year in which the selectmen considered contributing to the erection of a statue in honor of the British Prime Minister, William Pitt, Earl of Chatham, who had governed the British Empire during the French and Indian War. Though the selectmen of Medfield concluded that "to imitate Pitt as a patriot will be of more honor to him than the erection of a statue." Their high regard for him demonstrates just how British the colonists of Massachusetts remained after five generations in New England. And this *after* the Stamp Act Riots in Boston! Even ten years later, after the start of the American Revolution, a cousin of Noah Jr. named his son William Pitt

---

[1] See Chart I for the Allens of Medfield and Pomfret

Allen—a son who unfortunately, would be murdered by his "eccentric and somewhat foolish brother-in-law, Ebenezer Mason, who assisted about the farm work. One day in the spring of 1802 as the two were at work in the field laying out manure from a cart preparatory to planting, Mason became offended, and struck Allen on the head with the shovel he was using."[2] Mason was "tried, convicted and hanged on the 7th of October. Sometime prior to November 1st, Allen's body was stolen from the burying ground; a committee… reported that Sprague of Dedham and Zadock Howe, of Franklin, took the body; but the principal witness, Royal Sales, being concealed, they failed to prosecute the case."[3]

As we were saying, Sarah (Gay) Allen lived to see her son, Noah Jr., take her husband's place in the Allen Place. She lived to see Noah Jr.'s youngest son, Phineas Allen, march off to join General Washington's army. Phineas' father's second cousin, Capt. Sabine Allen, was instrumental in rallying the men of Medfield, and Phineas was at West Point during Benedict Arnold's treachery, and suffered with Washington's army in the Jerseys. At the end of the war, in 1782, he walked home hundreds of miles "in miserable plight." It was the year in which his grandmother, Sarah (Gay) Allen, aged ninety, died.

Succeeding his father at the Allen Place, Phineas was elected Selectman in Medfield in 1811, 1812, and 1822. He was Deacon of Medfield's Church (which had become Unitarian), and as a grandfather, he enjoyed frightening his grandchildren with tales of the Indian's attacks on Medfield during King Philip's War.

---

2   History of Medfield, William Tilden, 1887, pg. 304
3   Ibid.

Upon his death, his second son, Ellis, succeeded Phineas at the Allen Place. Three other sons he had sent to Harvard College.

Phineas' eldest son, Joseph, graduated from Harvard in 1811. Two books tell us a great deal about him and his world: his own *History of the Worcester Association* and his children's *Memorial*.

In his senior year at Harvard, Joseph Allen and his chum, Thomas Prentiss—the son of Medfield's minister—roomed in Harvard Yard in the northwest corner of the third story of Stoughton Hall, #9. Phi Beta Kappa kept its library in Stoughton and Allen was its librarian. For their graduation in 1811, the family and friends of Allen and Prentiss left Medfield for Cambridge in carriages at 4:00 a.m. They numbered twenty-five in all—a number larger than the number of graduates—and carried the feast to be eaten to the graduate's rooms before the commencement ceremonies. Black waiters walked from Medfield to serve this meal.

Joseph Allen was dressed for his graduation in knee britches and black silk stockings tied with ribbon at the knee, a black coat and ruffled shirt—all of which had been made at his father's house, while his pumps were made by the town's shoemaker. In old age, he recalled seeing at these early commencements, elderly gentlemen in wigs and tri-corn hats and buckled shoes with gold-headed walking sticks.

After the feast in their rooms, the graduates donned their classical robes and escorted their company to church for the disputations. Allen disputed with Morey (the son of Walpole's minister, who had studied Virgil with Allen in preparing for Harvard's entrance exam) on the question: "Whether the climate of any county has undergone a permanent change;" Allen taking the affirmative.

Edward Everett was the star of the Allen's class." He far outstripped all competitors in the race. He was first in the classics, first in Metaphysics, first in Belles-lettres, beyond all comparison the best writer and the best scholar. The first oration was assigned—*nemine contradicente*—to Everett, so perhaps none of Everett's classmates were surprised that he went on to become Governor of Massachusetts, United States Senator, President of Harvard and Ambassador to the Court of Queen Victoria. Even as a student at Harvard, President Kirkland remarked that Everett resembled the bust of Apollo. And in old age, the Rev. Joseph Allen could remember how the young Everett's hair "inclined to red and fell in graceful ringlets over his shoulders."

Everett began his public career as a Unitarian Minister, just as Joseph Allen had. In the year before Allen and Everett were admitted to Harvard, the college had taken one of the most momentous turns in its history. Dr. Ware of Hingham, suspected of being a Unitarian-Armenian heretic, was put forward for the Hollis Professorship of Divinity. Harvard had always been Calvinist-Trinitarian, and its President declared that he "would sooner cut off his hand than lift it up for an Armenian." He died, however, and in the next year, 1805, the overseers of the college met in the council chamber of the State House in Boston and—over the protests of the Calvinists—elected Dr. Ware to the professorship. In 1806, a Unitarian was chosen as President of Harvard, and in 1807 Everett and Allen entered the college.

After graduating from college, Allen stayed on in Cambridge studying divinity with Dr. Ware. During these years he lived in Holworthy Hall with a pleasant study opening upon Harvard Yard. Upon the completion of his studies, he married Dr. Ware's eldest daughter Lucy, and became Unitarian Minister in Northboro, Massachusetts—a position he retained until his death fifty-seven years later.

As a college student, Allen spent his winter recesses teaching. He used to say he "acquired his love for flowers while private tutor to the family of Mr. Theodore Lyman at his beautiful estate in Waltham." In Northboro, Allen kept a school for boarders in his home, and was superintendent of the town's public school. His was the first flower garden in town and was for many years a source of delight to the children of the place—Allen never wearying of supplying them with seeds and roots for their own cultivation. The inscription on his tombstone closes with the words, "a lover of flowers and little children."

Everett, as Governor of Massachusetts, created the first state Board of Education and appointed Horace Mann the state's first Secretary of Education. Allen was a correspondent of Mann's and one of Allen's pupils became a tutor in Everett's family. Allen's nephew, Nathaniel Topliff Allen, the son of his brother, Ellis, was both a student of his Uncle Joseph in Northboro and a teacher there. Nathaniel went on to become a protégé of Horace Mann, and Mann's first "model school"—the prototype for the American public school system—was the school Nathaniel Topliff Allen founded in West Newton. It was non-sectarian and co-educational, with a kindergarten and gymnasium. Today, it is a historical landmark.

The liberal avant-garde of the day considered Prussia foremost in the march of progress, and as a young man, Edward Everett had studied there. Horace Mann had made a study of Prussia's asylums and Nathaniel Topliff Allen spent two years as an agent of America's National Board of Education there.

Nathaniel Topliff Allen served as the principal of his school in West Newton for forty-eight years, employing numerous brothers, nephews, cousins, daughters, and uncles in the enterprise. His father, Ellis, an early abolitionist, retired there and must have been gratified to notice, from his rocking chair in the shade of the school's great ionic portico, that there were colored children among the student body. At his death, Ellis was eulogized by one of the most famous—or infamous—of the early abolitionists, William Lloyd Garrison. Garrison had suffered from the mob in Boston and been imprisoned in the South. He was an early supporter of women's suffrage, and refused to take his seat at the Anti-Slavery Conference in London when America's women delegates were not admitted. He was an early teetotaler. His devotion to these causes, together with his public burning of the Constitution and condemnation of New England's Church as a bulwark of slavery, alarmed the squeamish. But of Ellis Allen, Garrison wrote, "I shall always hold him in remembrance as one of the tried and true of the old 'guard of freedom', whose feet were planted on the everlasting rock,…who was ready to stand in the gap according to the exigency of the hour, and whose faith and courage never faltered as to the triumph he happily lived to witness."

In 1848, while Everett was President of Harvard, the Rev. Joseph Allen of Northboro was honored by the college with a Doctorate in Divinity. Harvard had changed since the two old friends had been students there—and not for the better. Everett, who had only lately been Ambassador to the Court of Queen Victoria, and a guest of the Queen's at Windsor Castle, now found himself debating with a worried Harvard faculty about what was to be done with students who threw chestnuts at Professor Ware (Allen's brother-in-law) during lecture. One morning at prayers, when many students showed evidence of having colds, President Everett remarked solemnly that, "In England gentlemen never blow their noses whereupon the entire college used their handkerchiefs in a most obstreperous manner."[4]

---

[4] Three Centuries of Harvard, Morison, pg. 277

In 1849, the year after Allen received his honorary Doctorate, he was chosen as a delegate to the Paris Peace Conference. Stopping in England, he called, in Hampstead, on Joanna Baillie "whose name and writing I had been familiar with for thirty years...She talks beautifully of Channing and the influence of his writing and life..." In the Lake County he calls on Miss Martineau after tea, but "unfortunately she had left home about a week before." He meets a Dr. Carpenter at Miss Baillie's, who is the son of Dr. Lent Carpenter, Miss Martineau's teacher. A Dr. Kinder has introduced him to Miss Baillie and Dr. Kinder is an associate of Lucy Aiken, the old friend of Channing—Dr. William Ellery Channing—the friend of Wordsworth. In the Lake Country, taking his umbrella against the rain, Allen walked "through a romantic region, two miles" to Rydal Mount, intending to call upon Wordsworth, only to find there was not enough time in which to call and get back for the omnibus to the railway station.

In Paris, the Minister of Foreign Affairs fetes the peace delegates at his "magnificent house" and "directs that the fountains at Versailles should play on Monday out of respect for the (Sabbitarian) principals and habits of the English and American Delegation." There is no evidence that Dr. Allen recognized the Foreign Minister as the Author of *Democracy in America*, M. Alexis de Tocqueville!

Besides Joseph Allen, two other sons of Phineas graduated from Harvard. One known as Silas, but registered at Harvard as William Winthrop Allen, graduated in 1817. While studying Divinity, he went insane, and was cared for first in Medfield at the Allen Place, then at his brother's in Northboro, then for a time at the first insane asylum in America in Worchester, until finally he "led a sometimes wandering, but harmless, and not unhappy life to extreme old age, dying in Medfield, in 1888, at the age of ninety-three."

The third son of Phineas Allen to graduate from Harvard was Phineas Jr. Graduating in 1825, he remained a teacher throughout his life, and the little we know concerning him, tantalizes. How one wishes Phineas Jr.'s own children had memorialized him, as his brother, Joseph's children memorialized their father!

Phineas Jr. studied Spanish at Harvard while Professor Tichnor—the mentor of Prescott!—was delivering his famous lectures on Spanish Literature. Tichnor's *History of Spanish Literature*—a monument of New England Scholarship—was based on these lectures. Tichnor, too, had studied in Prussia as a young man, with Edward Everett, so he knew what real scholarship was. While in Europe, he had visited General Lafayette and Lord Byron and Goethe and the young Pretender's Dutchess of Albany. Were there countless anecdotes about these personages shared with his pupils? Did Phineas share none of these anecdotes with his children? Were they unworthy of memorialization?

In the year Phineas entered Harvard, 1821, Ralph Waldo Emerson graduated and stayed on in Cambridge studying divinity. When Emerson moved to the old Manse in Concord in 1834, Phineas was already the Principal at the Concord Academy and Secretary of the Concord Lyceum, where Emerson would first display his native genius. Emerson's step-grandfather, Rev. Ezra Ripley—still a resident in the Old Manse—was the Lyceum's president. He had baptized Henry David Thoreau, who would later withdraw from Ripley's church with a protest as solemn as Luther's protest. It was Phineas who prepared Thoreau for Harvard at the Concord Academy. Were there *no* anecdotes here?

And again, in 1836, when the Concord Academies proprietors—the Hon. Samuel Hoar being chief among them—grew disgruntled with Phineas' anti-Masonic political agitations and dismissed him, were there no anecdotes worth recording? Phineas, after all, had taught Judge Hoar's children, Elizabeth and Ebenezer Rockwell Hoar. Elizabeth, the fiancée to Emerson's brother, the companion of her father on his quixotic mission to South Carolina, and the girl who filled Concord's Old Manse with flowers to greet the newlyweds, Nathaniel and Sophia Peabody; and Ebenezer Rockwell Hoar, a founder of the Republican Party.

Phineas was replaced as Principal of the Concord Academy and Secretary of the Lyceum, by a former pupil, newly graduated from Harvard: Henry David Thoreau; but, despite the disfavor of the academies' proprietors, Phineas went on to be elected Concord's town clerk. In our last glimpse of him, he was teaching Spanish at his nephew's school in West Newton. It is there in West Newton, in the winter of 1851–52, that Nathaniel Hawthorne, in the house of his brother-in-law, Horace Mann, wrote of his adventures among the Transcendentalists at Brook Farm in *The Blythdale Romance*.

But here, lest the impression be given that all of the Allen's of Medfield were (mere) Harvard graduates, ministers of religion or professional educators, we may note that a brother of the founder of the Allen School in West Newton, Joseph Addison Allen, recorded in his manuscript history of the Allen family that he could lift 900 pounds with his bare hands, while his brother, George, was the strongest man in Medfield and his brother William, the swiftest. Talents inherited, no doubt, from their great-grandfather, Noah Allen Jr., 1719–1804, who matched himself, according to the *Memorial*, in a tug-o-war with a pair of farm horses and broke a new cart rope and vaulted over cows at the age of eighty.

And yet, among the sons of Rev. Dr. Joseph Allen of Northboro, there were still more Harvard graduates. His eldest son, Joseph H. Allen, was ordained pastor of the church in Jamaica Plain when the venerable John Quincy Adams was on the ordaining council. Later, he lived in Cambridge and was editor of the Unitarian Journal, *Christian Examiner*, filling its pages with his writings: a sermon preached in Washington on the day following the funeral of John Quincy Adams; "A Sign of Terror" preached in June 1856 during the Troubles in Kansas; Comte's *Religion of Humanity; Prospects of American Slavery; The New Homeric Question*; and Weiss's *Life of Theodore Parker*.

Of another son of the Rev. Dr. Joseph Allen, Thomas Prentis Allen, it is recorded in the *Memorial* that, upon learning of his election to Harvard's Hasty Pudding, some years after his graduation, his eyes filled with tears.

While another son of the Rev. Joseph Allen, William, taught at Antioch College in Ohio, where Horace Mann had been the founding president and where there were lady professors. This William, no doubt, is the William Allen mentioned by Hawthorne in the journal he kept at Brook Farm. He was called upon, after Sherman's devastating march through South Carolina, to "reorganize" the schools of Charleston. His niece, Gertrude, a daughter of Thomas Prentis Allen, accompanied him, and, at age seventeen, taught a large class of Negro children for three months before dying of typhoid—"lamented by her pupils who saw her in visions as a celestial saint and heaped her grave with roses."

Chapter 2

James and John Allen: The Founding Generation

Uncle Augustus, in his *Brief History of the Allen Family*, writes that the Allen's were entitled to a coat-of-arms. "It was understood," he writes, "and believed in the family of the author's father...that the coat-of-arms in his branch of the Allen family was a 'winged spur' indicating great speed over all obstacles... awarded to one of my ancestors for delivering important news, in time of great peril, with unusual speed. My mother gave me from time to time in early life, the reported facts as above stated, and I have found a coat-of-arms apparently identical, connected with the Scotch Earldom of Hartwell and Marquisate of Annandale—dormant titles since 1792. What facts further researches may reveal remains to be seen. I have mentioned this subject in order to attract the attention of friends or relatives who may desire to obtain further information in relation thereto."

In encouraging "friends or relatives... to obtain further information" about the Allen coat-of-arms (a coat-of-arms giving the Allens a claim to the dormant Scotch Earldom of Hartwell and

Marquisate of Annandale?) perhaps Uncle Augustus remembered his own boyish excitement in 1820, when his father's cousin, Bulkeley Grosvenor, had prepared to set sail for England to claim the fabulous wealth and titles of the Grosvenor's of Eaton Hall, Chester.

In cousin Bulkeley Grosvenor's case, the facts, as ascertained by Uncle Augustus, were these: "About 1818, the head of the English Grosvenor family died, leaving the heirship and succession to title and great wealth to pass into the possession of a younger branch of the family...Bulkeley Grosvenor, one of those in the direct line of rightful succession, prepared to go to England to claim the property. But in December, 1820, when ready to embark for England, he was taken sick and died."

Family piety forbids a doubt concerning the merits of Uncle Augustus' "asertained facts." And my Grosvenor cousin's kindness to me during my stay with them in Pomfret in 1976 inspires my gratitude. Yet it must, nevertheless, be mentioned that the *Encyclopedia Britannica,* eleventh edition, contends—even as it exposes the genealogical obfuscations practiced by the so-called "English-Grosvenor's"—that the head of this English family lived from 1767 to 1845 and was succeeded by his son and grandson, which, *if true,* would mean that, in fact, there was no death of the head of the English family "about 1818," and thus alas—no inheritance of his fortune by a "younger branch" to be contested by Cousin Bulkeley Grosvenor.

When I consider Uncle Augustus' hint that the Allen's might have a claim upon the dormant Earldom of Hartwell and Marquisate of Annandale, I want to urge the bravest and brightest young relatives to set forth and seize upon what is rightfully theirs. But, it is well to know, in preparing for such adventures, the weak as well as the strong points in one's campaign. And,

The Founding Generation

in considering Uncle Augustus' evidence concerning the Allen coat-of-arms, it may seem peculiar, to some, that it was his mother—and not his father—who gave him the "reported facts" about this coat-of-arms. It may seem odd that the significance of the "winged-spur"—indicating the delivering of important news over all obstacles with great speed—should be remembered in such detail so many years later, when the knowledge of the line of ancestors, to whom these arms belonged, had disappeared.

But I have found a way around these vagaries. The great Samuel Eliot Morrison, in his *Founding of Harvard College*, wrote that the Rev. John Allen, first minister of Dedham and uncle of James Allen of Dedham and Medfield, was "the son of Reginald Allen, gentleman, of Colby, Norfolk." Reginald Allen's coat-of-arms (gentlemen by their very nature having a coat-of-arms) can be ascertained by an inspection of the herald's visitation records and compared with the arms of the Earls of Hartwell, putting an end to the question raised by Uncle Augustus. Though of course the Allen's might well be the descendents of some Domesday Book barons and their coat-of-arms much more ancient than the arms of the relatively upstart Earls of Hartwell. On the other hand, it must be pointed out that Roger Thompson, in his book, *Mobility and Migration*, concludes that the Rev. John Allen of Dedham is ***not*** the son of Sir Reginald Allen of Colby. A conclusion, he tells us, based upon a "private communication"; a "private communication" impugning the honesty and scholarship of the renowned historian, Samuel Eliot Morrison. Who are we to believe?

What is known concerning John and James Allen is that they came to New England during the Great Puritan Migration from England, and that they would have preferred to stay at home in England, but felt compelled to leave for religious reasons. The

Rev. John Allen, in his book *Defense of the Answers Made Unto the Nine Questions,* writes that "only the hope of enjoying Christ's ordinances" could have persuaded the emigrants to "forsake dearest relations, parents, brethren, sisters, Christian friends, and acquaintances, overlooking the dangers and difficulties of the vast seas, the thought thereof was a terror to many, and… go into a wilderness where we could forecast nothing but care and temptation."

    As a curate in Wrentham and Rector of Saxlingham, John Allen's Bishop was Matthew Wren of the Diocese of Norwich. Wren wished to establish the notions of church order approved by his king, Charles I, and the King's Archbishop, Laud. He wanted communion tables restored to the east end of the church. He wanted railings separating these tables from the laity. He wanted his clergy to wear a white surplice, and to bow at the name of "Jesus." The Puritans among his clergy, however, far from seeing these things as "Christ's Ordinances," considered them to be so many attempts at snuffing out the gospel-light in England and restoring the Whore of Babylon to her throne there. Forty ministers in the Diocese of Norwich were disciplined for resisting Bishop Wren's ordinances and fourteen emigrated. John Allen was one of these fourteen. Corbet, Bishop Wren's Chancellor, wrote that he wished Allen and his kind would rush over a precipice to destruction; "all percipitate with their percipitate and silly inventions," like the Gadarene Swine.

    Though the Rev. John Allen wrote of the many loved ones the emigrants left behind in England, he traveled with his wife, a son, a sister and brother-in-law. His brother-in-law, Thomas Fisher, had relatives married to relatives of the Rev. John Fiske who also traveled with them, along with his wife, mother, several brothers' families, numerous servants, tools for carpentry and husbandry, and provisions for three years in the wilderness.

"That excellent man, Mr. John Allen," Cotton Mather writes in his *Magnalia* "came aboard" the ship "in disguise to avoid the jury of their persecutors; but once they were past the land's end, they", Allen and Fiske, "entertained the passengers with two sermons every day, besides other agreeable devotions, which filled the voyage with so much of religion, that one of the passengers being examined about his going to divert himself with a hook and line on the Lord's Day, protested that he did not know when the Lord's Day was; he thought every day was a Sabbath Day; for, he said, they did nothing but preach and pray all day long!"

Once John Allen was settled in Dedham, he sent letters back to Wrentham in Suffolk—where he had been curate—encouraging its minister, John Phillips, to join him, and Phillips emigrated soon afterward. It is not known if John Allen's nephew, James Allen, emigrated with his wife in 1637, but if he did not, he emigrated soon afterward, for he was married in Dedham to Anna Guild on January 16, 1638.

When James Allen married, there was no minister in Dedham, for his uncle was not chosen minister until the following year. But for Puritans, marriage was a civic matter and no minister was necessary. This was one of the ways in which the religion of New England's Puritans differed from religion in England. Even after the eclipse of King Charles I, when friends of the Puritans were in power in London such differences continued to cause friction between Old England and New England. In his book, *Defense of the Answers*, the Rev. John Allen explains this friction as caused by the differing nature of church membership in the two churches. In England, the church traditionally included everyone, good and bad; but in New England, he explained, only visible saints—God's elect—were eligible for membership. In his *Treatise on Liturgy*, Allen wrote about the ordeal the New England Puritan suffered through before attaining the conviction that he belonged to God's elect. "The Lord knows," he wrote, "what prayers have been poured out to God by many alone, and in days of fasting and prayer, with God's servants together for consul, direction, assistance..." It took almost eight years of such "consul, direction and assistance" before his nephew, James Allen, could convince himself, and Dedham's Church, that he belonged to God's elect. But on September 2, 1646, James was admitted to Church membership. Only days later, as a Visible Saint, he was permitted to have his children baptized, and in the next year he took the Freeman's oath—for in the Massachusetts Bay Colony only Church members could be Freemen with a right to vote and a voice in public affairs.

As more and more Puritans arrived during the 1630s, the value of New England land and cattle increased dramatically. But in 1640 in England, the Puritan opponents of King Charles I assembled in the Long Parliament, and for twenty years England's rulers espoused a form of religion similar to that of New England. Emigration to New England nearly ceased, and some emigrants began returning to Old England. By 1641, Bishop Wren of Norwich and Archbishop Laud were prisoners in the Tower of London, and the Rev. John Allen's friend, John Phillips, could safely return to Wrentham in Suffolk as its minister. The Rev. John Allen's son, John Allen Jr., had emigrated with his father as a boy and graduated in 1643 with Harvard's second class. He returned to England, and the English authorities, ejecting a non-puritan incumbent, appointed him Vicar of Rye—Rye,

The Founding Generation

the village of Henry James and Lucia! In London, divines were meeting in Westminster Hall to discuss the form they thought the English Church should take. In an attempt to influence their decisions, the Rev. John Allen published his *Defense of the Nine Questions* in London in 1648. In the very next year, King Charles I was beheaded. The center of the Puritan world had moved from Boston to London; and the price of New England's land and cattle fell to half and then to a quarter of their value before 1640.

In 1651, two years after the King's murder, the town of Dedham formed a new town, Medfield, within its original borders. James Allen was one of Medfield's thirteen original proprietors; and in 1652 the last child of James Allen and Anna Guild, Joseph Allen, was born in Medfield. Back in Dedham, in the next year, 1653, James Allen's uncle, the Rev. John Allen, married the widow of Governor Dudley, and then was appointed an Overseer of Harvard College in 1654.

Events in England, in 1660, meant trouble for Puritans on both sides of the Atlantic. King Charles II took his seat upon the throne of his father, and John Allen Jr. was evicted from his vicarage in Rye, while Massachusetts' laws against Quakers and Baptists were threatened by the King's toleration. In 1668, five ministers, including the Rev. John Allen, had been ordered by Massachusetts' magistrates to engage several imprisoned Baptists in a public debate. After the debate, the Baptists were returned to prison, and the ministers warned the magistrates against toleration of the sect. But the King's toleration triumphed, and within two years Boston had its first Baptist Church.

Baptists and Quakers and Anglicans were not the only threats to Puritan New England; some were internal. In the 1660s, the Puritan's second generation were failing to enlist themselves among the Visible Saints. Half of Dedham's men were not church members, and, since only the children of church members could be baptized, the Puritan Church began to dwindle. At a Synod in Cambridge in 1662, the Rev. John Allen and his confreres devised a remedy—the Half-Way Covenant. It allowed the children of baptized parents, who were not church members, but who lived sober Christian lives, to be baptized. Meant as a solution to declining church membership, the Half-Way Covenant became instead a source of conflict between clergy and laity. In Dedham, Allen's congregation overwhelmingly rejected it. His last book, the *Animadversions Upon the Antisynodalia*, was a defense against Charles Chauncy's attack on the Half-Way Covenant.

The Rev. John Allen died in Dedham in the summer of 1671, leaving fifteen shillings to his nephew, James Allen of Medfield. Charles Chauncy—second President of Harvard—died in the following winter. James Allen died in Medfield in 1676. New England's founding generation was passing away.

Chapter 3

The Allen Family and the Sabine Family in Medfield and Rehoboth: The Second Generation

Of the seven children of James Allen and Anna Guild of Medfield, three married into the Sabine family of Rehoboth. The towns of Medfield and Rehoboth were less than thirty miles apart, and both were frontier towns. Most of New England's population lived to the east of these towns along the coast. While to the west, Medfield and Rehoboth were separated from the towns along the Connecticut River by the wilderness and its lurking Indians.

When James Allen's daughter, Martha, married William Sabine of Rehoboth, Sabine was a widower with twelve children—six of whom were under ten years of age. Martha (Allen) Sabine raised these children, even as she bore eight more of her own; ten years after Martha's marriage, two of her step-daughters,

Mary and Hannah Sabine, left Rehoboth and married Martha's younger brothers, Nathaniel and Joseph Allen of Medfield.

Rehoboth had been founded in 1643, six years before Medfield. Its proprietors had bought it from the Wampanoag Indian Chief, Massasoit—the same Chief who had helped the Plymouth colonists through their first winter and attended their first Thanksgiving—for ten fathom of beads and one coat. William Sabine's name appears with the other Rehoboth proprietors in the annual drawing of lots for additional woodland, meadowland and plain. In 1645, he and Capt. Richard Wright were elected to collect Rehoboth's taxes.

Contemporary documents describe William Sabine as Wright's "son-in-law," and their names often appear together in the town records. Wright was Rehoboth's principal organizer; and as agent for Col. Humphries, (whose wife, Lady Susan, was the daughter of the third Earl of Lincoln) Wright was an important man in New England. But William Sabine's first wife's name is unknown; and it is possible that "son-in-law" meant "step-son."

In 1646 and 1647, Rehoboth permits Sabine to erect a weir to collect herrings, to be sold at two shillings per thousand. (Twenty-five years earlier the Indian, Squanto, had taught the Pilgrims to use herrings in planting corn.) In 1648, Sabine is operating the mill formerly owned by Capt. Wright, and is charged by Plymouth Court with "not returning men's corn to them by two quarts to a bushel," but a jury clears him. (Capt. Wright left Rehoboth after a controversy over jurisdiction between Plymouth Colony and Massachusetts Bay Colony was decided in Plymouth's favor.) In 1653, William Sabine is grand juryman in Rehoboth, and authorized, with Capt. Miles Standish, to negotiate with Chief Massasoit over differences regarding land sold by Massasoit to the English. In 1655, Sabine is on a

The Second Generation

committee of seven authorized to levy rates to pay the town's minister, Samuel Newman. (Newman's gigantic *Concordance of the Bible* was probably taken by Capt. Wright to London for publication in 1643.) In 1656, Sabine is elected constable. In 1657, '59, '60 and '61, he is sent by Rehoboth as Deputy to Plymouth Colonies' Court. In 1663, he marries his second wife, Martha Allen of Medfield. In 1670 and 1671, he is Deputy again. By 1668, Chief Massasoit is dead, and his son, King Philip, now Chief of the Wampanoag's, signs a deed attesting to his father's sale of Rehoboth to the English. William Sabine's son, Joseph, is a co-signer of this deed.

About the time the first generation of English colonists, and the Indians who witnessed their arrival, began to die, New England's very existence was attacked; and the people of Rehoboth and Medfield took the brunt of these attacks. The immediate cause of these attacks took place on January 29, 1675, when John Sassamon, a former counselor of King Philip, was found dead—his neck broken, his corpse hidden beneath the ice on Assawomsett Pond—and some of King Philip's counselors were accused of the crime. When Sassamon's corpse was brought into the presence of the accused, it began to bleed afresh. William Sabine was the foreman on the jury which tried the accused; and, on the testimony of one eyewitness, the entire jury of twelve Englishmen and six Indians gave a verdict of guilty. The court sentenced the accused "to be hanged by the head until their bodies are dead," and King Philip's War was about to begin.

King Philip's warriors were encamped on a peninsula in Narraganset Bay just south of Rehoboth, and the first alarms—the night-time beating of the drums and the shrieking of the dancing warriors—could be heard in Rehoboth by Martha (Allen) Sabine, who was expecting her sixth child. Worse still, warriors from the Narraganset tribe in Rhode Island Colony, and the Nipmuck Tribe in the Massachusetts Bay Colony were joining with Philip's warriors.

Sassamon, before his death, had warned Josiah Winslow, Plymouth's Governor, that King Philip was plotting against the English. He had even expressed a fear that his warning might cost him his life. There had been other signs of trouble, too. Capt. Thomas Church, in his *History of Philip's War*, writes that Awashonks, the Queen Sachem of the Saconnet Indians "called her subjects together, to make a great dance, which is the custom of that Nation when they advise about momentous affairs." Capt. Church was himself invited, and riding to the place appointed, "found hundreds of Indians gathered together… Awashonks herself in a foaming sweat was leading the dance…" King Philip had sent six warriors to the dance "with their faces painted, with their hairs trimed up in a comb." Queen Awashonks told Capt. Church that Philip's warriors had given her a message: Unless she would join in his confederacy against the English, he would send his men privately to kill the English cattle and burn their houses, which would provoke the English to turn upon her. Capt. Church told the Queen he was sorry to see so threatening an aspect of affairs, and stepping to King Philip's men, "he felt their bags and finding them filled with bullets asked them what those bullets were for. They scoffingly replied, 'to shoot pigeons with'".

Philip's warriors started the war with looting and burning homes on the outskirts of Swansea and Rehoboth; and in this danger one of William Sabine's sons, Benjamin, left Rehoboth for the greater safety of Roxbury to the east near Boston. Another son, Jeremiah, was among the thousand soldiers sent against the Narragansett Indians in the first major English offensive.

The Second Generation

It was December, 1675, when these soldiers marched south into Rhode Island; the weather was cold and stormy; the troops had little protection from the elements; and those suffering from frozen limbs had to be left behind. On December 19, the English suddenly saw before them, emerging out of the gloom of a great swamp, on five or six acres of upland, a great walled Indian village. In all their experience with native construction, the English had never seen anything like it. At one corner the wall was incomplete, leaving a gap, and the first English troops to arrive rushed into it. Soon the village was an inferno of flame. It is not known how many Indians were killed or how many escaped. English casualties amounted to at least twenty dead and two hundred wounded. The English army—starving and freezing—retreated into the night. The battle became known as The Great Swamp Fight, and a month later the number of English dead was approaching seventy.

In the following month, January, 1676, Josiah Winslow led another thousand men against the Indians. This time another of William Sabine's sons, Samuel, was among the soldiers. The army chased the Indians over sixty or seventy miles and killed or captured a considerable number, but never fought a decisive battle. It became known as "the hungry march." The army had been forced to kill and eat some of its horses, and upon its return to Boston, it was disbanded.

One thing was now clear; diverse Indian tribes had now banded together against the English. But where would they strike? On February 21, 1676, the Nipmuck Indians attacked Medfield. "The sight of this poor people was very astonishing. The cry of the terrified persons, very dreadful," Samuel Newman, Rehoboth's minister, wrote to his friend, John Cotton, in Plymouth. The Indians had infiltrated Medfield at night, hiding in trees and barns "to take people in their first looking out of their doors in the morning." All who looked out were met with volleys of arrows and bullets. The fighting lasted most of the morning, as more and more Nipmucks jumped out from their hiding places. As some Indians shot down the English in their doorways, others were busy setting fire to their houses and barns. Driven out by smoke and flames, still more townspeople were killed. Fifty houses were destroyed and thirty inhabitants were killed or taken captive.

James Allen, the emigrant-founder of the family, died in Medfield in the year of the Indians' attack. His son, James Jr.'s house was burned to the ground. Three years before the attack, James Allen's son, Joseph, had married Hannah Sabine—the girl raised by his sister, Martha (Allen) Sabine—and at the time of the attack, she was expecting their first child.

Joseph Allen was a cooper by trade, and the Indians took wood shavings from his workshops and set them afire on his house floor. But this fire, being set upon a trap door leading to the cellar, fell through as it burned, and the flames were extinguished. All other buildings in that part of town were destroyed. The men of Medfield, to warn the people of Dedham, fired a cannon, and at the second firing, a panic seized the Indians and they fled across a bridge over the Charles River, setting it afire to stop the soldiers from following them. On a hill across the river, in full view of Medfield's smoking ruins, they roasted an ox and held a savage feast. The English knew well what such a feast could mean to the poor captives who had fallen into the Indian's hands.

On one of the posts of the bridge, the Indians had left the following notice: "Know by this paper, that the Indians that thou have provoked to wrath and anger will war these twenty-one years

The Second Generation

if you will. There are many Indians yet. We come three hundred at a time. You must consider that the Indians lose nothing but their lives, you must lose your fair houses and cattle."

In Rehoboth, the relatives of Hannah (Sabine) Allen would have heard of the attack on Medfield with alarm. Some of Rehoboth's outlying farms had been early targets of the Indian's menaces, but it had undergone no full-scale attack. Then, on March 18, 1676, in the month after Medfield's devastation, the Indians fell on Rehoboth in force.

When the Indians attacked Rehoboth, William Sabine had lived there for over thirty years. His wife, Martha (Allen) Sabine, was the mother of six small children, the youngest being seven months old. Most of the inhabitants took refuge in a few garrison houses. Canonchet, Chief of the Narragansett, who had escaped from the Great Swamp Fight, led as many as 1,500 warriors and indulged in an orgy of destruction. They burned forty deserted houses and thirty barns. Sabine's mill went up in flames. John Kingsley, an eyewitness, described the attack: "They burnt our mills, wrecked our mill-stones, yea, our grinding stones, and what was laid in the earth they found, corn, fowls, killed cattle and took the hind quarters and left the rest, yea, all that day. They burnt cart wheels, drove away our cattle, sheep and horses."

Though most of Rehoboth had taken refuge in their garrison houses, William Sabine's son, Nehemiah, refused to leave his farm and was shot to death at home, leaving three small children. (Was Nehemiah one of those who thought they would be protected by reading their bibles?) "We are shut-up in our garrison houses," Kingsley reported, "and dare not go abroad to our outlands... Ah, the burden that I bear night and day to see the blessed and loving God thus angry and we have not a prophet to tell us how long, and to say this or these are New England's sins."

That night, the Indians camped outside Rehoboth, and the English in their garrison houses could see their campfires. In the morning, at daylight, the Indians rose up and crossed the Pawtucket River to destroy Providence. "Nearly all that was English had been destroyed. It was a landscape of ashes, and farms laid waste, and corpses without heads. A place where three-legged cattle wander aimlessly, dragging their guts after them, and Indians strut through the woods wearing belts of human skin and necklaces of rotting fingers".[5]

No war in American history inflicted casualties on a greater percentage of the population. Several thousand people lost their lives; families were scattered; homes and life savings vanished beyond hope of redemption. The devastated New England towns did not recover their prosperity for a hundred years. On the list of the ninety-three Rehoboth inhabitants who advanced money to the town to defray the costs of King Philip's War, William Sabine advanced more money than all but two. He lived another twelve years.

How then did New England survive? Why were the English not driven back into the Atlantic from whence they had come only a generation earlier? Why did New England recover and thrive while its Indian enemies declined? Capt. Church offers clues to this puzzle in his *History of Philip's War*.

Even before the war began, Church had advised the Queen-Sachem Awashonks not to fight against the English. He wanted her warriors to fight with the English, with him as their captain. But before this could happen Church needed a commission as

---

[5] *The Name of War*, Jill Lapore, 1998

The Second Generation

captain of such a joint English-Indian force from the Governor in Plymouth. On his way to seek such a commission, on July 20, 1676, in Rehoboth, "he was offered a guard to Plymouth, but chose to go with ***one man only who was a good pilot.***" About sunset, he, with SABIN, his pilot, mounted their horses at Rehoboth, where the army now was, and by two hours by sun next morning, arrived safe at Plymouth. The Governor agreed to Church's request, and in less than a month, Church's joint English-Indian force ambushed King Philip. Philip "fell on his face in the mud and water... a great, naked, dirty beast." Church gave his head to "the Indian who shot him, to show to such gentleman as would bestow gratitude upon him; and accordingly he got many a penny by it".

CHAPTER 4

THE DANIEL ALLEN SR. FAMILY IN POMFRET AND HIS MARRIAGE TO HANNAH DAVIS: THE THIRD GENERATION

JAMES ALLEN WAS THE FATHER of Joseph Allen, and Joseph was the father of Daniel Allen—the third generation of Allens to decorate Armena (Allen) McLellan's family tree. Whole branches of Daniel's family remained in Medfield and its vicinity for centuries, but Daniel—born in Medfield on April 21, 1681—moved west to the northeast corner of Connecticut. In 1703, when he is first mentioned as living in Connecticut, he is twenty–two years old. Two uncles had preceded him there. In 1686, when Daniel was only five years old, his mother's brother, Benjamin Sabin, had been among the first thirteen English pioneers to settle this corner of Connecticut; and five years later, in 1691, John Sabin, another of Daniel Allen's uncles, also settled there. (This John Sabin, as a half-brother of Benjamin Sabin and

Hannah (Sabine) Allen, and a son of Martha (Allen) Sabine, was both uncle *and* cousin to Daniel Allen.)[6]

A letter written by Uncle Benjamin Sabine, in 1703, to Connecticut's Governor, Fitz-John Winthrop, gives us our first evidence of Daniel Allen's presence in Connecticut. The letter mentions him as among those men living near Woodstock, in Windham County, and needing "defense on account of the Indian troubles."

The Sabine and Allen family had suffered from Indian troubles before, in Massachusetts in King Philip's War. At that time, Uncle Benjamin Sabine had moved his family away from the frontier at Rehoboth to the safety of his wife's family's town of Roxbury near Boston. They had been safe there, while the Sabine's who remained in Rehoboth were either besieged in their garrison houses or murdered like Benjamin's brother, Nehemiah.

Benjamin Sabine had three children when he moved from Rehoboth to Roxbury, and eleven years later, in 1686, he had nine—the sixth named after his brother, Nehemiah. In that year, 1686, Roxbury's Selectmen determined that their population could no longer be supported within their town's limits and petitioned the General Court for a tract of land in the Western Wilderness seven miles square. Scouts with Indian guides set out on the Connecticut Indian Trail to reconnoiter, and found suitable land in present-day Woodstock in Connecticut. Negotiations were opened to purchase this land with Capt. James Fitch, for the Mohegan Chieftain, Owaneco, had entrusted Fitch with the land's sale. The document—signed by Owaneco with the pictograph of a bird in 1680—reads in part: "Others taking advantage of me when I am in drink, I make over my

---

[6] See Chart II

The Third Generation

right and title of any and all my lands and meadows, unto my loving friend, James Fitch, Jr., for him to dispose of as he shall see cause." Only five years earlier, Owaneco and his Mohegan Warriors had joined with the English to chase King Philip. He had been with the English at the Great Swamp Fight.

Just as soon as Capt. Fitch gained control of Owaneco's land, he offered it for sale. Personal interest as well as the public good led him to dispose of the Indian's vast tracts of land to good and substantial settlers, rather than to speculators. Roxbury town was the first to buy from him, and when its purchase was complete, Benjamin Sabine, Daniel Allen's uncle, was among the first thirteen pioneers to make the trek west. Another of those first thirteen pioneers was Matthew Davis—the uncle of Hannah Davis. Of her we read, in Woodstock's records, about nineteen years after the purchase of Woodstock from Owaneco, on July 11, 1705, "Daniel Allen of Mashamoquet" (This is Benjamin and John Sabine's nephew, living in Mashamoquet or Pomfret on Woodstock's southern border) "entered his purpose of marriage with Hannah Davis of Roxbury" (the niece of Matthew Davis). So, both Daniel Allen and his wife, Hannah Davis, had uncles who were among Woodstock's first thirteen settlers.

The Davis family had lived in Roxbury, Massachusetts since at least 1643, for the birth of the first child of William Davis—the progenitor of this family in America—is recorded in that year. In 1653, Davis was granted a house lot; and in 1660 he owned land beyond Muddy River, within Boston's bounds, abutting Roxbury. An early member of Roxbury's church, William Davis' death is noted in its records in the hand of Elliot, the Apostle to the Indians. At the time of his death, Davis had already given land at Muddy River to his son, Joseph, Hannah's father. Three years after his death, his son Matthew—Hannah's uncle—set out with Roxbury's first pioneers to found Woodstock in the western wilderness.

On arriving at Woodstock, Matthew Davis, Benjamin Sabin and the other eleven pioneers built a shelter and saw to the laying out of roads. They kept watch at night against bears, wolves and Indians. They distributed land and formed committees to implement their plans. Matthew Davis and Benjamin Sabin were prominent on all these committees.

In Roxbury, the minister Eliot noted the "week we sent out our youth to make the new plantation." Woodstock was some eighty miles from Roxbury, and the last thirty of those miles were through untouched wilderness. On arrival, the pioneers broke up the land and planted it. They built a shelter big enough to house both themselves and some thirty more families who were expected at the end of the summer. There would be no time then to plant food and build houses. On August 18, the additional families arrived, and "after solemn prayer to God the disposer of all things," the assembled colonists drew lots for land. Benjamin Sabin drew a lot for twenty acres on the west side of Plaine Hill, where the first pioneers had built their first shelter; and Matthew Davis received sixteen acres nearby. The settlers named the stream they had followed to Woodstock, "Muddy Stream," after Muddy River near Roxbury where the Davis family had their farms.

In his diary on March 13, 1690, Judge Sewall in Boston wrote, "I gave New Roxbury the name of Woodstock because of its nearness to Oxford for the sake of Queen Elizabeth…" (In England the village of Woodstock stood near Oxford, and Queen Mary had once confined the bastard Elizabeth there.) Just two years later, Judge Sewall would be defending Salem Village against the attacks of Satan and his witches.

The Third Generation

At Woodstock's first town meeting in 1690, Benjamin Sabin was chosen one of the five selectmen in whose hands were placed "the whole power of the town, except granting land and admitting inhabitants." At the same meeting, Sabin's house was chosen as a watch house. In 1691, he was chosen "to oversee the works of a road to Providence, Rhode Island," the nearest metropolis. In the same year, Jonathan Davis—another uncle of Hannah—was chosen constable. When the meetinghouse was completed and a minister secured, Benjamin Sabin was chosen Deacon. All goes well, but for Indian threats and alarms. The French enemy to the north was stirring up their Indian allies against New England.

In 1690, even as Benjamin Sabin was being chosen one of Woodstock's first Selectmen, his elder brother, Samuel of Rehoboth, was setting sail from Boston Harbor with New England's fleet on a crusade against the French. (Was Sylvanus Davis—an English prisoner in Quebec—a relative of Hannah Davis?)

As the fleet approached the great fortress of Quebec, Samuel Sabin, a sergeant in the crusade, would have been struck by a large image of the Holy Family hanging from Quebec's Cathedral Spire. Outraged by this popish idol, the English wasted a considerable part of their scanty powder and shot in an unsuccessful attempt to hit it. When they had exhausted their ammunition, they had no choice but to retreat. The French ascribed their victory to the Holy Virgin, and her image was carried in procession from church to church. Quebec's commander wrote to his king asking for a few squadrons that he might punish the insolence of the English by crushing them in their den of Boston. In Boston, all was dismay. In their retreat, many English had died of cold, small pox and fever, while the crusade had burdened Massachusetts' Treasury with a debt of fifty thousand pounds.

In 1696, the war between the English and French had so inflamed the Indian problem, that Mohawk warriors attacked Woodstock's neighbor, Oxford. So disturbed was Woodstock by this that its public affairs, roads and fences were neglected. Its millhouse fell into dilapidation, so that "bad weather did often spoil the corn," and Deacon Sabin and Matthew Davis were sent by the town to treat with Mr. Bartholomew, the mill-wright, who promised "as soon as it was good weather, to set the mill in good repair." (In 1699, Hannah (Davis) Allen's maternal uncle, Edmund Chamberlain Jr., would marry this millwright's daughter.)

When Roxbury purchased Woodstock from Capt. Fitch, an additional purchase of 15,000 acres on Woodstock's southern border was also made. Called Mashamoquet by the Indians, it would become the township of Pomfret, and Benjamin Sabin was among its first thirteen purchasers. Only the Indian menace delayed its settlement. Huddled together in their garrison houses in Woodstock, Pomfret's purchasers feared to take possession. Only one man had the courage to cross the line from Woodstock into the Pomfret wilderness in that time of peril: Cap. John Sabin, a younger half-brother of Deacon Benjamin Sabin and Hannah (Sabin) Allen, the son of Martha (Allen) Sabin and William Sabin. He had purchased a hundred acres in Pomfret from Capt., now Major, Fitch in 1691 for nine pounds and built a fortified house on his acres before the Indian attack on Oxford in 1696. The local Indians had been scattered by King Philip's War, and on returning to their native haunts, found the English settling there. Called Wabbaquasetts, and usually friendly, these Indians could sometimes be persuaded to join the Mohawk's bloody forays. In those dangerous times, Capt. John Sabin gained influence and authority over them. Though alarms and panics were frequent, and some settlers returned to Roxbury, Capt. Sabin held his ground. He had been only ten years old when he watched from a garrison house in Rehoboth as the Indians burned the town and destroyed his father's mill. Now, he had a garrison house of his own to defend.

A letter written in 1700 to Gov. Fitz-John Winthrop of Connecticut, from the Earl of Belmont, Massachusetts' Governor, summarizes Capt. Sabin's brave service. "I have been made sensible of the good service done by Mr. John Sabin... He having created that confidence in the Indians of his friendship as to be trusted with their secrecy; and that during the late troubles and war he did, at his own great charge and expense almost to the ruining of his estate, subsist and succor a considerable number of Wabbaquasetts within a fortification about his own house, whereby, he not only prevented their defection but also rendered them serviceable to the English... I cannot but account it very impolite to lose so useful and public spirited a man, or that he be discouraged by ingratitude, much more by injustice. I pray in his favour, that you will effectually recommend his services and expenses to the consideration of your General Assembly for a suitable recompense to be made to him. I shall not fail to endeavor some gratification for him from this government..."

In the years that followed the writing of this letter, relatives of Deacon Benjamin Sabin and Capt. John Sabin began to follow them from Massachusetts to Connecticut. In 1701, Daniel Sabin, an orphaned son of their brother, Nehemiah, marries in Windham, a town adjacent to Pomfret. In 1703, Deacon Sabin writes Gov. Winthrop about his nephews David and Daniel Allen—sons of his sister, Hannah (Sabin) Allen who live south of the Woodstock line and are in need of defenses against the Indians. By 1704, the Indian menace is subsiding, but scouts are still maintained in the woods; Woodstock's first school is built, and Deacon Sabin arranges the seating order for the church. In the next year, Deacon Sabin and his six sons leave Woodstock and move south to his land in Pomfret.

In Pomfret, Deacon Sabin took a leading role in the town's establishment just as he had in Woodstock. His name heads the list of petitioners seeking recognition and incorporation of Pomfret in 1713. He is a member of the committee to choose a minister and to provide an ordination dinner for forty persons. In 1719, he is Pomfret's first representative to Connecticut's General Court; and in 1725, his is the second corpse to be buried in Pomfret's new burying place. In 1705, the same year Deacon Sabin left Woodstock for Pomfret, on July 11, Woodstock's Vital Records include an entry stating that Daniel Allen of Mashamoquet (Pomfret) entered his proposal of marriage to Hannah Davis of Roxbury.

The relatives of Daniel's mother, Hannah (Sabin) Allen, and their early influence in Woodstock and Pomfret, find parallels in Hannah Davis' family. Her sister, Abigail Davis, marries Deacon Benjamin Sabin's son, Jeremiah in Pomfret, forming another link between the Allen, Sabin and Davis families.[7]

Her maternal grandfather, Edmund Chamberlain, moved from Roxbury to Woodstock, and his son married Woodstock's miller's daughter in 1699, while another son, Edmund Jr., had died in the Great Swamp Fight. After the death of her father, Joseph Davis, and her brother, Joseph Jr.—both of whom died in December of 1717 and were buried in the same grave—all five of Hannah (Davis) Allen's nephews (Joseph Jr.'s sons) moved

---

[7] See Charts II and III

to Woodstock. Matthew Davis, Hannah's uncle and one of Woodstock's pioneers, moved south to Pomfret in 1731.

Extensive researches have failed to discover the parents of William Davis, the founder of the Roxbury family, but because his son, Deacon Ichabod of Roxbury, embellished his will with a red wax seal representing a griffin sergeant, some suppose the Davis' of Roxbury are descended from David Davis of Caermarthen in Wales, a lineal descendent of King David of Wales, a descendent of King David of Jerusalem.

My own favorite Davis relatives are Capt. William Heath Davis and his son, William Heath Davis Jr.[8]

Capt. Davis—a great-grandson of Hannah (Davis) Allen's brother, Joseph Davis Jr.—entered the China trade in 1807, when he cleared the vessel *Mercury* out of Boston Harbor. He traded Boston's manufactured goods in Alaska, California's horses and hides in Hawaii for sandalwood, and sandalwood in China (where they burned it for incense) for silk, tea and porcelain. Settling at last in Hawaii, he married Hannah, the eldest daughter of King Kamehameha's governor of Oahu, Oliver Holmes—a governor whose servants wore loincloths and served roast dog. His son, William Heath Davis Jr., settled in California and married Maria de Jesus Estudillo of Rancho San Leandro, writing in his old age the memoir, *Seventy Five Years in California* about the unsurpassed felicity of life in Mexican California.

In the summer of 1972, on the fast train from Milan to Avignon, I met the Hon. Samuel Pailthorpe King, who had just run as a Republican for governor of Hawaii. Mentioning the

---

[8] See Chart III

fact that my ancestress, Hannah (Davis) Allen's brother, Joseph Davis, had decendents who settled in Hawaii, Pailthorpe King exclaimed, "You don't mean to say that you are descended from *the* Hannah (Davis) Allen, whose nephew, Joseph Davis Jr., had a son, Joshua Davis, who kept an inn in Woodstock, Connecticut? Whose son, Amasa, was Massachusetts Quarter Master General during the Revolutionary War? And whose second son, Maj. Robert Davis, was a member of the Boston Tea Party—whose own son, Capt. William Heath Davis, settled in Hawaii?"

"Well, yes…"

"Dearest Cousin!!! I am descended from Capt. Davis' daughter, Charlotte Holmes Davis!"

In the following autumn, Pailthorpe King sent me copies of a photograph of Capt. Davis and his Polynesian consort[9] made from glass negatives preserved in King's family. There had been no need, I felt, to share with King the letters of Capt. Davis' niece, Adelaide Dana—courtesy had constrained me. For in those letters Adelaide expatiates upon Capt. Davis' "immorality," "the disgrace he brought on his family," "his infamy" and "illegitimate offspring." But, perhaps a place might be found in a footnote to our chapter on our Dana ancestors to treat these charges with the impartial historical analysis they deserve.

---

[9] See picture on next page.

The Third Generation

Hannah and Capt. Davis

Chapter 5

Daniel Allen Jr. marries Mary Adams: The Fourth Generation

From 1670 to 1700, Connecticut's population increased by fifty-eight percent. From 1700 to 1730, it increased by 280 percent. The flood of immigrants spilling into the region came from towns in southeastern Massachusetts incapable of supporting their younger generation. Capt. Fitch's Indian land found eager buyers. Population pressure on Roxbury was so acute that its men had bought two entire townships from him—Woodstock and Pomfret.

Two of Hannah (Sabin) Allen's brothers—Benjamin and John Sabin—were, we have seen, prominent among the early pioneers on the trek from Massachusetts to Connecticut. Two of her sons—Daniel and David Allen—followed their uncles, while a contrary, if much smaller, movement of population saw a return from the Connecticut frontier to the older settlements in Massachusetts. Among these were four of Deacon Benjamin

Sabin's children who left Woodstock-Pomfret in Connecticut to settle in Medfield, Massachusetts, where the Deacon's two sisters, Hannah (Sabin) Allen and Experience (Sabin) Bullin, could be counted upon to welcome them. The youngest of these children, Stephen, had been born in Woodstock, and accompanied his father on his move to Pomfret; but in 1716, at the age of twenty-seven, he appeared in Medfield as a schoolmaster. His aunt, Experience (Sabin) Bullin, and her husband, being childless, had given him their farm in exchange for maintenance for life. Stephen's brother, Nehemiah, had preceded him to Medfield, but when he decided to return to Woodstock, Stephen took possession of his farm too. More than ten years before his arrival in Medfield, two of Stephen's sisters had left Woodstock, about the time their father was moving to Pomfret, and married in Medfield; Experience (a niece of Experience (Sabin) Bullin) married David Morse-the maltster and Deacon; and Sarah, married Dr. Samuel Adams.[10]

Like the Allen's and Sabin's, various members of the Medfield's Adams family moved west to Windham County, Connecticut. Dr. Samuel Adams' brother, Joseph, left Medfield in 1721, to settle just south of Pomfret in Canterbury Township. A cousin from Medfield—one of the innumerable Henry Adams's—had also settled there. All three—Dr. Samuel, Joseph, and Henry—were first cousins of President John Adams' grandfather.

---

[10] The record of Samuel Adam's death in the town records lists him "Doctor." His tombstone lists him "Mr." and in the settlement of his sister's estate in 1704, he is called "cordwainer" or shoemaker. Some of his recipes for medicines have been found in the old memorandum book. A potion to relieve strangury—painful urination—advises: "take nine bees and put them into beer alive 'till they die, and drink that beer in the morning."

The Fourth Generation

At the time Joseph Adams left Medfield, his eldest child, Mary, was sixteen years old. On November 12, 1728, at age twenty-three, she was married in Pomfret to Daniel Allen Jr. As a girl in Pomfret, she would have known her husband's grandmother, Hannah (Sabin) Allen, who did not die until 1730, and many of his aunts and uncles. Fifty-two years before this marriage, Lydia Adams, a cousin of Mary's father, married her husband's great uncle, James Allen II. Uncle Augustus Allen, in his *Brief History of the Allen Family*, states that "by intermarriages we are connected with the Adamses"; but nowhere in his book does he record them.[11]

The facts are these: Mary Adams' father, Joseph, was the son of Peter Adams, who moved to Medfield from Braintree in 1652. Peter was the son of Henry Adams of Braintree, the founder of the family.

In honor of this founder, John Adams, the second President of the United States, erected a granite column in the cemetery at Braintree carved with these words:

> *"In memory of Henry Adams who took his flight from the DRAGON PERSECUTION in Devonshire in England, and alighted with eight sons near Mount Wollaston. One of the sons returned to England, and after taking time to explore the country, Four Removed to MEDFIELD and the neighboring town… this stone and several others have been placed in this yard, by a great-great grandson, from a veneration of the Piety, Humility, Simplicity, Prudence, Patience,*

---

[11] The uninitiated—queasy with the kaleidoscopic richness of these lineages—must consult charts IV and V.

Temperance, Frugality, Industry, and Perseverance of his ANCESTORS, in Hopes of Recommending an Imitation of their virtues to their POSTERITY."

In 1840, the son of President John Adams, John Quincy Adams, the sixth President of the United States, wrote to a distant Adams relative: "About forty years ago Elijah Adams of Medfield, one of the descendants of the Patriarch, collected and formed a genealogical tree of all the male descendants to the fourth generation... Elijah Adams, of Medfield, the author of the round robin genealogy of the family, dedicated his work, of which he had a high opinion, to my father, then President of the United States. Elijah was a plain country farmer, with only a common school education, who deemed it no inconsiderable illustration of the family that he himself had obtained the dignity of a Justice of the Peace. His knowledge of the world was not very extensive, but he had taken great pains, and made profound researches in the town and parish records of Medfield, Boston, Medway, Stoughton, Mendon, Chelmsford, and others, as well as Braintree, to gather the names of all the male progeny of the patriarch, Henry. Among the rest he addressed himself to **His Excellency**, Samuel Adams, the governor of the Commonwealth of Massachusetts, who underrated all genealogies as much, perhaps, as Elijah over-valued them. He told Elijah that he knew nothing of his ancestors beyond his own father, that he had never made any inquiries concerning them for fear of finding that some of them had been perhaps **too much exalted**, with a significant gesture to explain that he meant the exultation of the gallows. I shall never forget the astonishment with which Elijah more than once related this anecdote to me... My own father was not thus indifferent to his ancestry, nor distrustful of them. There was no reason for such distrust. They were humble in life, farmers and mechanics, and whatever memorial remains of them was blameless... Should you visit the Commonwealth of Massachusetts according to the purpose mentioned in your letter, and find it suits your convenience, I shall be happy to see you at my house."

Thirteen years later, in 1853, in the January issue of the *New England Historical and Genealogical Quarterly,* an article appeared, "Of great interest to every American": A genealogy "copied from an ancient parchment roll with arms" demonstrating that Henry Adams, the founding patriarch of Braintree, was "of the sixteenth generation from Ap Adam, who came out of the Marches of Wales at a very remote period about six hundred years ago. An engraving of a Gothic window, accompanying this article is described in a note by Charles Francis Adams, Jr.—grandson of President John Quincy Adams:

In the upper part of a Gothic window on the southeast side of Tidenham Church, near Chopston, is the name JOHES Ab Adam 1310, and his coat of arms: sergeant on a cross gules five mullets or. All of which are still (1851) to be found, beautifully executed in stained glass of great thickness and perfect preservation." The article states further that John Ap Adams was summoned to parliament as a Baron, and Uncle Augustus repeats this statement in his *Brief History*. No doubt he would have embellished his history with a copy of the Adams' coat-of-arms, if he had been able to give an exact account of their intermarriages with the Allen's. Alas! Only years after the discovery of this "ancient parchment," it was shown to be a forgery.[12]

---

[12] Henry Adams, the historian and great grandson of President John Adams, invents Norman Ancestors, in his ***Mount-Saint-Michel and Chartres***, to assuage himself for the loss of this Barony.

Today, it is known that Henry Adams, the Patriarch of Braintree, was a farmer in the village of Barton St. David, Somersetshire; that his wife, Edith Squire, was from the neighboring village of Charlton Macknell, on the River Cary; and that they arrived in Boston about 1636 with nine children. In James Truslow Adams' book, *The Adams Family*, he writes that the patriarch, Henry Adams "was granted land at Mt. Wollaston, afterward called Braintree, and managed to establish a foothold. After his burial on the eighth of October, 1646, the inventory of his estate reveals that he had a house and barn, a cow and a calf, some pigs, furniture and utensils, and three beds—one in the parlour and two in the chamber. More noteworthy, and probably relics of the old days in England, were a silver spoon and some old books. The estate was worth about seventy-five pounds, equally divided between real and personal property. He had done his work well."

The patriarch's son, Peter,[13] the grandfather of our own Mary, married Rachael Newcombe of Braintree before removing to Medfield. Rachael had sailed from England in 1635, on the *Planter*, with her parents and grandparents when she was 2½ years old. Her mother, Rachael (Brackett) Newcombe was the sister of Boston's jailer, Richard Brackett, who would succeed Henry Adams as Braintree's town clerk. The Brackett's and Newcombe's were members of the largest kinship network yet uncovered among the participants in the Puritan's Great Migration. More than forty immigrants were related to them by blood or marriage **before** their immigration.

Peter and Rachael (Newcombe) Adams were members of a little colony of Braintree people who were among Medfield's

---

[13] See Chart B

The Fourth Generation

first settlers. They lived near one another on Bridge Street in Medfield, and in King Philip's War they suffered as the Allen's had suffered. Peter's house was burned to the ground. His brother, Edward—later to serve as Selectman and town representative—lost his house, too. Their brother, another Henry—Medfield's miller and leader of its militia—was shot dead in his doorway. His wife escaped to the house of the minister, where soldiers were quartered, but a few hours after the Indian attack, a soldier's gun discharged accidentally and killed her in an upper chamber. The house of her married son, Eleazor, was also burned to the ground.

The Indian's attack on Medfield came in the morning of February 21, 1676. Thirty-three years later, in 1709, Peter Adams' son, Joseph, becomes a member of Medfield's church. In 1713, Joseph and his brother, Peter Jr., were petitioners to divide the township of Medfield, so that the land on the west bank of the Charles became the town of Medway. The first preaching service in that town was held in Peter Jr.'s house, and it is said he called the people together by the old drum that he had brought back from the Indian Wars. In 1720, Joseph Adams held town office; and in 1721, he sold his house, barn and land on the Dedham Road, a few rods beyond the stone mill, to Dr. James Gerauld, and moved his family to Canterbury, Connecticut. His eldest child, Mary, was born in 1705, and was sixteen years old when they left Medfield-Medway. When she married Daniel Allen Jr. in Pomfret, just north of Canterbury, her memory of his relatives in Massachusetts would have been quite strong.

The records with which we reconstruct this outline of the lives of Daniel Allen Jr. and his wife, Mary Adams, are public record—colony records, township records and church records—records as scant, in the case of Daniel Jr. and Mary, as they are for any of their ancestors. Among these records, and enumeration of their nine children will be found—the fourth child, Ebenezer, being born in Pomfret in 1737—Ebenezer, the great-grandfather of Armena (Allen) McLellan.

In the midst of these dry records, it is tantalizing to discover that there was once a family portrait of near relatives of Daniel Allen Jr.—a painting of Mrs. Peter Chandler (Daniel's sister's sister-in-law) and her daughters, painted by her husband's cousin, Winthrop Chandler. Unfortunately the great-grandchildren of Mrs. Peter Chandler "unconscious of her portrait's ancestral value, wore it 'out in play.'"[14] How precious it would have been as an example of the valiant beginnings of the arts in America!

The Chandlers,[15] like the Sabin and Davis families, were among the first pioneers from Roxbury to immigrate to Woodstock. The founder of the family, John Chandler, was, with Benjamin Sabin, a Deacon of Woodstock's first church. His son, Capt. Joseph Chandler, inherited the Deacon's land in Pomfret; and Capt. Joseph's land was inherited in turn by his son, David Chandler, who married Mary Allen (the sister of Daniel Allen Jr.), and Peter Chandler, whose wife and daughters were painted by his cousin, Winthrop Chandler.

The painter, Winthrop Chandler, was a grandson of Judge John Chandler, who was himself another son of the founding Deacon Chandler. The Judge was an assiduous surveyor for Capt. Fitch when the Indian lands were first being sold; and his elegant 1719 map of Pomfret Township is much decorated by his elegant script with the names of Pomfret's first proprietors: Benjamin and John Sabin, John and Joseph Chandler, and—to skip ahead—the three brothers, Jacob, Benjamin, and Daniel

---

[14] See *Art in America*, April 1947
[15] See Chart VI

The Fourth Generation

Dana—brothers about whom more will be found in the following chapter, where we shall find Ebenezer Allen, the child of Daniel Allen Jr., marrying Mehetabel Dana, the granddaughter of Daniel Dana, in 1760.

But this date—1760—reminds us that we approach the date of the American Revolution. Peter Chandler, fortunately, commissioned cousin Winthrop Chandler to paint a depiction of the Battle of Bunker Hill—a depiction that, in 1847, remained intact in the family of his great-grandson's widow, in a house on Plain Hill in Woodstock, where the first pioneers from Roxbury had built their first rude shelter.

It is not known *how* Winthrop learned to paint. Like so many of New England's first artists, he may have found his way into the presence of Smibert's copies of Old Masters in Boston, and been seduced by the muse there. He died penniless.

CHAPTER 6

THE MARRIAGE OF EBENEZER ALLEN AND MEHETABEL DANA

On the survey map of Pomfret drawn up by Capt. Chandler in 1719, the names of the landowners—Benjamin and John Sabin, John and Joseph Chandler, and the three Dana brothers, Jacob, Benjamin, and Daniel—are elegantly inscribed upon their respective properties. Some forty years later, on December 10, 1760, Mehetabel Dana married Daniel Allen Jr.'s son, Ebenezer, in Pomfret. There had already been several intermarriages connecting the families of the bride and groom. Mehetabel (Dana) Allen's great-uncle Jacob Dana[16] married Patience Sabin, a sister of her husband Ebenezer's great-grandmother, Hannah (Sabin) Allen. A daughter, Hanna Dana, of this same great-uncle had been married in Canterbury to Henry Adams II, the first cousin of Joseph Adams of Canterbury—Ebenezer Allen's great-grandfather! While Benjamin Dana, another of Mehetabel's great uncles, had had a daughter, Ann,

---

[16] See Chart IX

who married Matthew Davis, Jr., the first cousin of Ebenezer Allen's grandmother, Hannah (Davis) Allen.[17]

Mehetabel was the granddaughter of Daniel Dana; and Daniel and his brothers were the children of Richard Dana of Cambridge, the immigrant. Born in Manchester, England, and baptized in its Collegiate Church (now Manchester Cathedral) in 1617, Richard was the son of Robert Dana, a tanner who lived "in the Mylnegate" in Mill Street. In 1624, Robert was one of the two sworn "Bylawmen for Milngate"—officers charged with keeping the "mastidogs and bitches and great mungrell curs," that go abroad in the streets, chained up continually or "musled."

By 1640, Robert's son, Richard, was in Cambridge, Massachusetts—1640, the very year in which Henry Dunster (who had kept a school near Manchester) sailed to New England and was elected President of Harvard College. Dunster had encouraged friends and students to join him in New England, and Richard Dana may have been one of his students. Judge Sewall, whose father also lived on Mill Street in Manchester, writes in his diary of Richard Dana as "Father Dana."

In 1647, Richard Dana received land from Massachusetts' General Court—over one hundred acres, across the Charles River from Cambridge Town in what was then called Little Cambridge, now Brighton. Ascending the Charles from Boston Back Bay, one passed first, on the right or North bank, Cambridge town, then Watertown, then farther up, on the left bank, Dedham, and finally Medfield. Dana's farm stood on the bank opposite and between Cambridge and Watertown. It started at a place on the river called "the Pines"—the first point up river where the

---

[17] Chart IX

The Marriage of Ebenezer Allen and Mehetabel Dana

banks were high enough on both sides for a good opportunity to land at all times—an early place chosen for a ferry.

On the southwest edge of Dana's farm was a great oak—famous as the place where the Apostle Elliot preached to the local Indians in their own language. For almost thirty years these Christian Indians were friendly neighbors of Dana; but in 1675—amid the terrors of King Philip's War—they embarked at Dana's landing place, "the Pines" (near what is now the corner of Western and Brighton Streets), and were transported down the Charles to Deer Island in Boston Harbor, where they starved and froze through the winter.

Not long after Dana moved to his farm, he married Ann Bullard, a daughter of Robert and Anne Bullard. Ann had emigrated in 1635, as a child, with her parents to neighboring Watertown. (J. Gardner Bartlett has traced the Bullard's ancestry back five generations in his *Bullard and Allied Families*.) From this marriage, Dana, who had been one of eleven children, became the father of eleven children. In 1654, he presented a modest gift of cotton cloth to Harvard College as a contribution toward the repairs of buildings destroyed by fire, while other donors gave cash and cows. Sixteen fifty four was the year in which Henry Dunster resigned as President. In 1661, at a town meeting in Cambridge, Dana was chose to act as Constable. In 1663/64 he was chosen Viewer of Fences, and in 1665, Surveyor of Highways. In 1678, and 1680, Dana was one of the tithing men on the south side of the river, and as such, was required to see that all persons observed the Sabbath, attended public worship, and paid attention during the sermon. In 1678/79, 1683 and 1689—the year before his death—he was appointed to the Grand Jury in the Court of Assistances, which met in Boston and was presided over by the Governor.

Even after a new church was founded in Little Cambridge, Dana remained faithful to the church in old Cambridge, crossing the river each Sunday with his wife and children from his landing place near "the Pines." The children, born in Little Cambridge, were all taken across the river and baptized at the First Church. On April 2, 1690, Judge Sewall records in his diary, "Father Dana falls from a scaffold and dies." He was seventy-three years old, and fifty of those years had been spent in Cambridge—it is probable that he was buried in the old burying ground opposite Harvard College, where several of his sons and numerous later descendants were buried. Of his three sons who purchased land in Pomfret, two, Benjamin and Daniel, and Daniel's wife, Naomi Croswell (the grandparents of Mehetabel Dana) are buried in the same old burying ground.

Naomi Croswell's mother was Priscilla Upham, daughter of John Upham, who, with twenty-one other families, had sailed with the Rev. Joseph Hull from Weymouth, England, in the Great Puritan Migration.[18] In Massachusetts, the General Court granted a plantation to these emigrants at the south end of Boston Bay and named it Weymouth. The place had already been settled by non-puritan English companions of Capt. Robert Gorges—years before the arrival of Winthrop's fleet; and when the Rev. Hull refused communion to some of Weymouth's earlier inhabitants, they invited Robert Lenthall to be their minister, for he had rejected New England's innovation of asking people to give a testimony of spiritual regeneration before being admitted to church communion. One of Hull's parishioners, Masakeill Bernard, wrote back to Old England informing his father, the Rev. Richard Bernard of Batcome, Somerset (Roger William's

---

[18] See Chart C at front

The Marriage of Ebenezer Allen and Mehetabel Dana

father-in-law), about the ensuing controversy. The Rev. Bernard wrote a critique of the Puritan's idea of church covenant, and the Puritans of New England responded with a book co-authored by the Revs. Allen of Dedham and Shepherd of Cambridge (Richard Dana's minister), *The Answer Made Unto the Nine Questions*.

Bernard was well known in godly circles. Having named a son, Masakeill, (from the Hebrew captions to psalms sometimes interpreted to mean an instructive or meditative ode), one is not surprised to learn that he veered briefly into separatism, binding a hundred Christians from his flock and neighboring parishes in a covenant, but since that time, he had been an implacable opponent of separatist churches, with the fervor of one who has seen the error of his ways. But his daughter Mary's husband, Roger Williams, was New England's arch separatist. In Boston, John Cotton had to protect the New England way from both Bernard, the anti-separatist, and Williams, the arch-separatist, while Bernard accused him of being tainted with the same errors as his son-in-law.

Gov. Dudley, hearing of a possible outbreak of small pox at Weymouth, commented, "If this be true the plague is begun in the camp for The sin of Peor" (a biblical allusion to unlawful mingling with the ungodly). Things looked bad for Weymouth, but the magistrates intervened. Lenthall was persuaded by various ministers to accept the General Court's ruling and leave. One of his backers was fined. One, being penniless, was whipped. The policy of the Bay Colony was a simple one—those who would not conform should be silent or leave.

It was in these exciting times, from 1636 to 1639 that John Upham served as Weymouth's representative to the General Court. His daughter, Priscilla, was born in 1642, the very year in which her father was one of the commissioners for treating with the Indians in relation to lands in Weymouth; and then, between 1648 and 1650, the Upham family left Weymouth for Malden, a town near Charleston and Cambridge—a proximity which explains the marriage of his daughter, Priscilla, to Thomas Crosswell and the marriage of their daughter, Naomi Croswell, to Daniel Dana of Cambridge.

John Upham was Selectman and Deacon in Malden for more than twenty years. His gravestone there records the day of his death, February 22, 1781/82, at age eighty-four. His son, Nathaniel, was sometime minister at Malden, and another son, Phineas, was a deacon of the church. William, son of Phineas, married Naomi Dana, daughter of his cousin, Naomi (Croswell) Dana.[19]

Mr. Charles W. Upham, in the preface to his classic books on Salem witchcraft in 1867 writes that, "Every person desires to preserve the memory of his ancestors…" and it is he who made a pilgrimage to England and discovered the will of John Upham of Malden's father at Exeter, and discovered in the parish records at Holy Trinity Church, Exeter, the baptism of Phineas on September 21, 1634, son of John and Elizabeth Upham.

Daniel Dana and his wife, Naomi Croswell, were married before 1691/92. They lived upon land that had been granted to his father, Richard, and they had nine children. In 1689, Daniel served in the military on garrison duty. He was a cooper and farmer. In 1696/97, he and his wife were admitted to the church and remained esteemed members. In 1736, he was on a committee of "wise, prudent and blameless Christians" who acted as a privy counsel to the minister. He was tithingman in 1698 and 1700. In 1702, he was a surveyor of highways "to

---

[19] See Chart IX

join with Boston Prambulators." He was Selectman in 1715 and 1725. In 1718, his son Richard graduated from Harvard College. In 1728, he gave land for a schoolhouse. In 1733, a document is filed in Pomfret, Connecticut, in which Daniel deeds land there to his son, Ebenezer. Ebenezer is mentioned in Daniel's will in 1742. And, on October 10, 1749, Daniel Dana dies in his eighty-sixth year.

On November 16, 1738, five years after his father deeded him land in Pomfret, Ebenezer Dana, age twenty-seven, marries Mehetabel Goodell b: Pomfret on Mar 16 1716/17. Living in Pomfret Township, they were surrounded by Ebenezer Dana's cousins, the children of his uncles Jacob and Benjamin. By 1733, there were four schools in the township. One of these was at the end of Samuel Dana's land. Samuel Dana was the son of Uncle Jacob Dana. Among the thirty-five original members of Pomfret's Union Library Association in 1739, are four Dana's, all styled Yeomen (Ebenezer was *not* one of them), and three Sabin's. All of the Library Association members covenant under their hand and seal "to pay a certain specified sum to be used and approved to purchase, procure, and buy a library." Uncle Jacob Dana's sons—Samuel, a blacksmith, and Jacob Jr., a cooper—had lived in the part of Pomfret Township called Abbington since 1722.

Nine children were born to Ebenezer Dana and Mehetabel (Goodell) Dana between 1738 and 1759. A beautiful glimpse is given into the early life of the parents of Mehetabel (Goodell) Dana in Ellen Larned's *History of Windham County*, Volume I, page 156. Their names were Thomas Goodell and Sarah Horrell, and of them Larned writes:

"The first settlement within the purchase limits (Pomfret) was prior to 1700. One of the first settlers was Thomas Goodell, who, after a brief sojourn in Woodstock, bought land of Deacon

Chandler in 1699. He is said to have come up alone to the new township to put up a house and prepare for his family—but that his wife became uneasy, took her spinning wheel in hand, and came to look for him in mid-winter, and by the aid of teams and chance, Woodstock travelers made the long journey in safety."

The records of church and town add a heightened poignancy to Larned's history for they show that Sarah Horrell was married to Thomas Goodell in Beverly on December 2, 1698, in the winter before her winter trek to Pomfret; that she was dismissed from Woodstock's Church to the Church in Woodstock in 1698; that in 1699 her first child was born—named Humphrey after her father; and that at the time of her winter trek to Pomfret, alone, in snow with her spinning wheel and baby (?) she was fifteen years old. Her daughter, Mehetabel (Goodell) Dana kept a pewter basin stamped with her parents' initials: G (Goodell) T (Thomas) S (Sarah). She was pleased, no doubt, to have a memento of such intrepid parents. The basin became a treasured heirloom in the family of Uncle Augustus—but *that* is another story.

Concerning Sarah (Horrell) Goodell's family, its founder, her grandfather, Humphrey Horrell Sr., was unlike the other ancestors we have already dealt with—indeed, he and his wife seem to have been unlike all of the other thirty great-great-great grandparents of Nathan Allen, in that he did not immigrate to Massachusetts. He is first recorded in Maine on March 11, 1650/51 when he is sued in Kittery Court. We may assume that he was one of the hard-bitten, adventurous, independent, non-puritan-sailor-fisherman-trader-farmers settled on Maine's coast. In the following year, Horrell sues William Norman in Kittery Court—on the very day Norman was banished for bigamy.

The Marriage of Ebenezer Allen and Mehetabel Dana

For many years, Horrell Sr. was associated with the men who developed Maine's Pemaquid-Damariscotta-Muscongus Peninsula. John Pierce, a merchant of London, had held the original New England patent under which the Pilgrims colonized Plymouth. John Pierce's son, Richard, was settled at Muscongus in Maine—in part, it might be, under a subsequent patent of his father and in part by purchase from the Indian sagamore, Capt. Somerset. (Capt. Somerset, of Maine's Pemaquid tribe is the same Indian—Samoset—who learned English from the fishermen of Maine, and astonished the pilgrims in Plymouth by greeting them in English.) Richard Pierce's daughter, Elizabeth, married Richard Fulford, and Richard Fulford sold Humphrey Horrell Sr. a tract of land at Muscongus, at the mouth of the river of that name, running two miles inland on October 21, 1667. Horrell's title to the land was evidenced by an endorsement on the original deed, which Fulford had from Samoset.

On this great tract, Horrell cleared a plantation, called "Withbarne," and farmed with the help of hired labor—including Richard Pierce's son, John. Until, ten years after his purchase, an Indian attack, in 1676, swept the English from the coast of Maine. King Philip had already been defeated in Massachusetts when Maine's Indians began killing and capturing the English there. At first, Horrell, his wife and companions, took refuge in the fortified village in Pemaquid Harbor. When that refuge proved untenable, they ferried in small boats to the Demaris Cove and Monhegan Islands, and were evacuated from there by ships to towns in Massachusetts—the Pierce's and Fulford's taking refuge in Salem and the Horrell's in nearby Beverly. In the next year, 1677, in the adjacent town of Marblehead, the ladies of the town tore two captured Indians from Maine into pieces.

Humphrey Horrell Sr.'s son, Humphrey Horrell Jr., (the child-bride, Sarah Horrell's father) was a sailor. In 1692, when Sarah was a child of eight, her father was in command of the sloop, *Sea Flower,* of Beverly (twenty tons burden, no guns, two man crew, plantation built), which cleared from Portsmouth, New Hampshire for Boston with a cargo of 6,000 red oak staves and 3,000 feet of boards. From what is known of Humphrey Jr.'s father and the English settlements in Maine, it seems probable that he was either born in some English port or in one of Maine's fishing hamlets, and was early sent to sea as an apprentice or ship's boy. He seems not to have been with his father at the "Withbarne" plantation between 1667 and 1676, for the elder Horrell hired the boy, John Pierce, to help there with the plowing. He is not listed as having been in military service in King Philip's War, or later, and this, with the long gaps between the recorded births of his children in Boston, may indicate that he was away on oversees voyages much of the time before he came to Beverly in 1687. For in 1687—after the death of his parents and his first wife, Sarah—Humphrey Horrell Jr. was married in Beverly to his second wife, Elizabeth Smith. She raised Humphrey Horrell Jr.'s two daughters by his previous marriage and bore him four more children.

In 1728, a claim was entered on behalf of Humphrey Horrell Sr.'s heirs, with the Eastern Claims Commission of the Massachusetts General Court, for the two miles of land on the Muscongus River owned by Horrell. The claim was entered by Elizabeth (Smith) Horrell's second husband, Deacon Samuel Sturtevant of Plympton. Yet, to this day, nothing has been done to abate this injustice. One cannot help but think of the claims to land in Maine of Hawthorne's mother's family and his House of the Seven Gables!

The Marriage of Ebenezer Allen and Mehetabel Dana

Humphrey Horrell Jr. died in 1710, but his widow did not remarry until 1715. It was during the five years of her widowhood that her two stepdaughters married. One of these, our own ancestress, Sarah Horrell, married Thomas Goodell, a relative of her stepmother. Both Sarah Horrell's stepmother and Sarah Horrell's husband were grandchildren of Robert Goodale (see chart VII). Her husband, Thomas, was the son of Thomas Goodell, a son of Robert; and her stepmother was the daughter of Elizabeth (Goodell) Smith, a daughter of Robert.

About Robert Goodale, the founding emigrant of the Goodell family, the stupendous tomes entitled *The Great Migration* record that he "was an interesting character who did not fully participate in his community, but who, throughout his half-century of residence in Salem, pursued a single goal with great determination. So far as we can tell, he was never a church member, never a freeman, and never an officeholder. The vast majority of the records in which he appears, even his few minor criminal transgressions..." (his cattle and goats, in the 1640s, were apt to wander into neighbors' cornfields. And he was accused by Michael Sallow of stealing four goats, which Sallow had found, with his mark on them, in Goodale's custody. Goodale promised to return them, but when Sallow went for them, Goodale said he had killed one and the rest were lost. (Perhaps they were in *his* corn.) "The vast majority of records in which he appears... involve his dealing with land. He devoted much effort to the amassing of land, and the provision of competent estates to his children."

Among the many men from whom Robert Goodale bought land, it is interesting to note his purchase of forty acres from Henry Herrick, the cousin of the cavalier poet Robert Herrick. (Could there be a more exquisite refuge from Puritan Salem than the limpid, lilting, lyrics of this poet?) Goodale also sells fifty acres to Giles Corey—the hero of today's witchcraft boosters. Corey's name also appears in court documents concerning the Goodale's. In 1672, before the birth of either Thomas Goodale or his child-bride, Sarah Horrell, John Smith (Thomas Goodale's uncle and the father of the Elizabeth Smith who would become Sarah Horrell's stepmother)[20] sued his sister-in-law Elizabeth (Beauchamp) Goodale, the mother of Thomas—who, however, was not yet born!

Elizabeth (Beauchamp) Goodale had complained of her brother-in-law, John Smith, a man married to her husband's sister. Giles Corey's wife, Mary, testified that Elizabeth had told her that once, when Smith "was working in a swamp near her house, he called to her for fire, so she carried it to him and laid it on the side of the brook. He asked her to tarry and smoke, and she told him she had already smoked, so she ran away up the hill and he ran after her… also at another time he assaulted her when he fetched her from her house to help his wife when she lay in, so that she jumped from the horse on which they rode. Also, when he was at Lot Kellam's" (another brother-in-law, married to a Goodale) "digging a well, and once on a Lord's Day while her husband was at meeting…She said he was an ugly rogue and threatened to tell her husband, and that he had been uncivil to her ever since her son Zachary was a little boy" (Her eldest child born in 1668.) "but she feared that if she told her husband, Smith would kill her or her children, or hurt her creatures."

Lot Kellam testified that his wife, Hannah Goodale, "being lame from a fall that she received upon a rock, John Smith offered

---

[20] See Chart VII

her abuse, and she told him of it at night. Whereupon, deponent dealt with said Smith privately."

Smith was suing Elizabeth for slander—but her plea was that "if common fame may be credited 'it is not a very easy matter to slander the plaintiff.'" The jury found Smith guilty and the court ordered him whipped on the next lecture day in Salem and to remain in prison until the sentence be executed unless he pay forty shillings. Upon supplication, Anthony Needham and Giles Corey, who engage to pay the fine and goal charges within two months, his sentence of being whipped was remitted.

Both Elizabeth's husband, Zachariah Goodale, and her brother-in-law, Lot Kellam, had deposed that Smith, "being at said Goodell's house the latter's wife being present, said that he was sorry for what he had done to Goodale's wife and prayed God to give him repentance, hoping he should do so no more. Zachariah replied that he wished God would give him repentence."

Twelve near neighbors of the Goodale's certified that "having had acquaintance with Elizabeth Goodale, the daughter of Edward Beauchamp, from her childhood to her marriage, according to our best observation and judgment, she hath been of an honest, civil, conversation and one that would not wrong the truth in her speeches."

Giles Corey and his wife had done what they could for Smith. Corey had been one of the men bound for Smith's appearance in court. He had testified that, at his house, Smith had affronted Elizabeth. Corey went up the ladder into the chamber and when he came down "he saw nothing but laughing and smoking. Elizabeth said she was like to have broken her brother Smith's head with the ladle and his (Corey's) wife said if she had there would have been but sixpence or a groat to pay."

Finally, Elizabeth states that, "The stories have been greatly exaggerated" having "come to the mouths of such talkers as have prevented the truth and made the matter appear far worse than even it was to my great scandal and reproach. Mary Cory and Mary Caril hearing it came to enquire of me how it was, and I foolishly told my pretended friends…" She went "downe the town to acquaint Major Hathorne with it." (Major Hathorne, ancestor of the Great Hathorne and a judge at Salem's witchcraft trials). "I desire if may be a warning to me and us all never more to jest or speak foolishly, vainly or slightly of such matters as should be cloathed with gravity and modesty, and I do acknowledge tis a dishonor to the sect of women… I desire that the truth should not be wronged nor yet that John Smith should suffer more than he hath deserved… The language John Smith used to me and the actions were such as most tend to the way of his calling in dealing with cattle and not so like unlawful dalliances tending to uncleanness."

Three years later, in 1676, Giles Corey and his wife were in court again with Zachariah and Elizabeth Goodale. Zachariah's brother, Jacob, a simpleton, thirty-four years old, had been beaten unreasonably by Giles Corey "with a stick of about an inch in diameter nearly a hundred times in the presence of Elisha Kebee, who told Corey that he would knock him down if he did not forbear." About ten days later, Corey went to the house of Zachariah Goodale, and told him that his brother, Jacob, had had a fall. He was afraid that he had broken his arm, and desired him to take Jacob to Mrs. Mole's in the town. Jacob, up to that time had been lusty, but now seemed confused and stooping and he was very pale and his eyes sunken. Thereupon Zachariah went to Corey's house, and saw Jacob, who was there. The roads were slippery, and Corey said that his horse was not caulked, so he could not

The Marriage of Ebenezer Allen and Mehetabel Dana

go with him. Jacob went so badly, Zachariah asked him if he had any other hurt than his arm, but he would not tell. Zachariah then requested that someone might go with them, for he would not go alone with him, whereupon Goody Corey went with them. Jacob died a few days later and an inquest was held. Lot Kellam deposed what Jacob told him upon his deathbed. The jury made the following report:

"We find several wrongs he hath had in his body as upon his left arm and upon his right thigh a great bruise which is very much swold and upon the reins of his back in color differing from the other parts of his body, we caused an incision to be made much bruised and run with a jelly and the skin broke upon the outside of each buttock."

For this abuse, Corey was fined.

In 1992, a memorial was erected to Giles Corey, on the site of what was Corey's farm—a granite stone inscribed with the words, "Witch Hysteria Martyr, Irascible, Unyielding Giles Corey DIED Under Torture of STONE WEIGHTS SEPTEMBER 19, 1692." Longfellow cast Corey as a martyr in his play, *Giles Corey of the Salem Farms* in 1868, and in William Carlos Williams' play *Tituba's Children*, Corey makes an appearance.

In the excitement leading up to Corey's execution for witchcraft, the girl, Ann Putnam, Jr., age 12, daughter of Sergeant Thomas Putnam, Salem Village's clerk, testified that she had seen Giles Corey's ghost, that it had "afflicted me by beating, punching, and almost choking me to death urging me to write in his book. I verily believe that Giles Corey is a dreadful wizard for since he has been in prison he or his appearance has come to me a great many times and afflicted me."

This deposition was taken on April 13, 1692. In the following September, before Corey is pressed to death on September 16,

Ancestor Worship

Thomas Putnam writes to Judge Sewall reporting that the ghost of Jacob Goodale has now appeared to his daughter.

"There appeared unto her (she said) a man in winding sheet; who told her that Giles Corey had murdered him... the Devil there appeared unto him, and promised him he would not be hanged... the apparition also said that her father knew the man, and the thing was done before she was born. Now Sir, this is not a little strange to us... for all people now remember very well... that about seventeen years ago, Giles Corey kept a man in his house that was almost a natural fool; which man died suddenly. A jury was impaneled, whereof several are yet alive, brought in the man murdered; but as if some enchantment had hindered the prosecution of the matter, the court proceeded not against Giles Corey..."

And, in fact, Giles Corey was not hanged, but pressed to death, as the Devil had promised him. He was over eighty-one years old, and as the weights were piled on, his tongue protruded from his mouth until the sheriff pushed it back in again with the end of his walking stick. He was the first—and last?—in New England that was ever pressed to death.

After their marriage, Thomas Goodell and Sarah Horrell, his bride who was fourteen and a half, leave Beverly and Salem. They leave the Atlantic Ocean where Sarah's father sailed his ships, and the village where the ghost of Thomas' uncle appeared to Ann Putnam. In Connecticut, in the wilderness of Pomfret Township, they build a farm and raise a family. From them, through five generations, an heirloom descends to the family of Augustus Allen. Since it is the most venerable tangible artifact—The Palladium and Penates—giving witness to the family history, (aside from the scribal jottings of Church and Court), Augustus describes it with some care in his *Brief History* on page 64:

The Marriage of Ebenezer Allen and Mehetabel Dana

"The heirloom in the Nathan Allen family (Augustus' father) is a pewter basin, holding about two quarts, with a turned over rim about half an inch wide, and having the following letters cut or stamped upon the bottom:

G
T S

The G stood for Goodell; T for Thomas, and S for the initial of his wife's name. This was then the customary way of placing the initials of husband and wife upon presents or keepsakes…

The accepted belief, as handed down with this basin from parent to child, has been that Nathan Allen's maternal ancestress came over on the Mayflower in 1620, and was the fourth woman who landed upon Plymouth Rock from that vessel; and that she married a Goodell; and history furnishes strong corroborative testimony, in connection with said 'heir-loom', that such belief was well founded. We find that Thomas Goodell was one of the first settlers in Mashamoquit, or Pomfret.

There is apparently no human reason for the careful preservation of that almost worthless pewter basin for so many years past, excepting a well founded belief in the truth of the statements made above."

Not content with this, Augustus returns to the subject of the Allen's Mayflower Heirloom on pages 71–73. There he writes "it is not at all surprising that 'the Mayflower ancestress' name is not mentioned in the list of passengers… We must depend more or less upon tradition and 'heirlooms,' as handed down from parent to child, for the history of our ancestress, Mrs. Goodale who came over on the Mayflower. Her name and history were, no doubt, well known to my grandmother... But, apparently, no record thereof was preserved."

And again, "It was, however, well known that grandfather Allen married Mahitabel Dana, as before stated, and that her mother's maiden name was Mahitabel Goodell, and it was the accepted report and belief that her grandmother came over on the Mayflower in 1620, and brought with her, among other things, a pewter basin and a copper warming pan, both of which have descended as heirlooms... Through all these years there has never been any question or doubt upon these points..."

And finally, on the last page (120) of his *Brief History*, Augustus conjures a picture of his twin brother—age eighty-six—"holding the 'pewter basin' of the Mayflower, the 'heirloom' of the Nathan Allen Family, carrying its history back for two hundred and seventy five years..."

Now, a plain statement of Uncle Augustus' contention is this:

His grandmother—Mehetabel (Dana) Allen—was the daughter of Mehetabel (Goodell) Dana. TRUE

Mehetabel (Goodell) Dana's paternal grandmother—Elizabeth (Beacham) Goodell—came over on the Mayflower. FALSE

I do not wish to be unsympathetic. There is a seriousness about Uncle Augustus' statements—a rapt persistence—that ought, I think, to be accepted with deferential politeness by those of us who, in after times, have benefitted from his labors—and I am one of them. There is even perhaps a sense in which his quixotic determination to possess a Mayflower descent was laudable. But I myself have so many Mayflower descents—and those from the best families on the ship, the Winslow's and Alden's—that it is, perhaps, difficult for me to imagine what it would be like to be without them. Perhaps Uncle Augustus felt that it was vaguely disreputable to be—like the Irish, Italians, and Mexicans, without one. Or perhaps he felt that a rich lawyer in New York City with an office on Wall Street and a farm in Poughkeepsie—a friend of the millionaires, Mr. Vassar, of Vassar College and Mr. Cooper of Cooper Union—deserved a Mayflower descent.

Was Uncle Augustus quite mad? Did he make it all up? Or did he have helpful hints from his mother? After all, her memory had retained the history of the Allen coat-of-arms so vividly; perhaps she had been able to make suggestions concerning the provenance of the "worthless Pewter Basin," too.

The truth is, however, that this worthless pewter basin came to the family from Augustus' grandmother, Mehetabel (Dana) Allen. It had belonged to her maternal grandparents, Thomas Goodell and Sarah (Horrell) Goodell, and it was stamped with their initials. Uncle Augustus was familiar with Larned's *History of Windham County*. If he had known that in Volume I, page 156 of this history, (where Thomas Goodell's young wife, in mid-winter goes alone with her spinning wheel in hand to find her husband in the wilderness of Pomfret) commemorated *his* ancestress, Sarah Horrell, perhaps he could have relinquished his "Mayflower heirloom" for her sake. Or if he had known that the Horrell's had been in Maine and had two miles of land on the Muscongus River that had belonged to Samoset, the friend of the Pilgrims, perhaps that might have helped. Perhaps he could have set his lawyer's mind to work on getting those two miles of riverfront returned to his family.

In order to quash even the most obdurate belief that one among our Goodell ancestors' wives was the fourth woman to alight from the Mayflower onto Plymouth Rock, let us take each of these wives in turn to test that belief. The first Goodell emigrant, Robert, was enrolled at Ipswich, England, for passage to New England on April 30, 1634, on the *Elizabeth*, with his wife, Kathern. Surely even Uncle Augustus would think it unlikely that this Kathern had also sailed on the Mayflower fourteen years earlier. The son of Robert and Kathern, Zachary Goodell, was baptized in Salem on May 31, 1640, and was married in Salem on December 31, 1666, to Elizabeth Beacham. Elizabeth did not come over on the Mayflower either, but was born in Salem in 1648, the daughter of Edward Beauchamp, who was received as an inhabitant there in 1636–37. The son of Zachariah and Elizabeth was Thomas Goodell, who as we have seen, married Sarah Horrell, whose family had come from Maine, not Plymouth. Thomas and Sarah were the possessors of the "worthless pewter basin" that was to become the Allen's "Mayflower heirloom"; and their daughter Mehetabel Goodale married Ebenezer Dana, whose ancestors in Cambridge and Pomfret we have already mentioned.

What I think has not been mentioned, is that Ebenezer Dana died on August 19, 1762, in His Majesty, George III's service, at the end of the French and Indian War, in Havana, Cuba. Ebenezer, and a son of his cousin, Isaac—Isaac Dana Jr.—had enlisted on April 1, 1762, in a company of soldiers led by Col. Israel Putnam, a neighbor whose farm was just south of Pomfret. Isaac Dana Jr., aged thirty-four, was Col. Putnam's aide-de-camp. Ebenezer Dana was fifty-one years old. The bounties the British government offered colonial soldiers were high. The French enemy was hated and French Canada had already been defeated. Col. Putnam had been with Amherst when Montreal capitulated without resistance.

King George III wanted peace, and entered into secret negotiations with the French. But it was discovered that the

The Marriage of Ebenezer Allen and Mehetabel Dana

Bourbon Kings of France and Spain had entered into "The Family Compact," so on June 4, 1762, England declared war on Spain. The Philippine Islands in the Pacific and Cuba in the Caribbean—far-flung outposts of the Spanish empire—were to be Britain's targets.

After enlisting in the campaign against Cuba in April, Ebenezer Dana made his will out on May 17, 1762—mentioning his wife, Mehetabel (Goodell) Dana, his son, Daniel, who is to receive two-sixths of the remainder of his father's estate—and four daughters, including his eldest daughter, Mehetabel, whose husband, Ebenezer Allen, is also mentioned. The Provincial troops arrive at Cuba between July 28 and August 2, 1762, having been preceded by British troops on June 7. Only the arrival of the Provincial troops allowed the British to bring their siege of Havana to a successful end. Heat, disease, scarcity of drinking water, and the evident impregnability of Havana's castle walls had taken such a toll on the British that it had become clear they would not have enough men left to storm the fort even if they could breach its defenses. But then the troops from North America arrived—including the men from Connecticut—and the city surrendered on August 14. The British laid hold of three million pounds of gold and silver, and most of Spain's Caribbean fleet—a quarter of the Spanish Navy. Ebenezer Dana died on August 19, 1762. At least half of the British soldiers who shipped out on the expedition died of wounds, yellow fever and other maladies. Ensign Miller, with the English Army at Havana wrote, "The bad water brought on disorders that were mortal. You could see men's tongues hanging out like a mad dog's…" The death rate was worse among the Provincials; of the 1,050 men in the Connecticut Regiment, 626 died before returning home—59.5 percent. France, England, and Spain signed the

Preliminary Articles of Peach on November 3rd. Isaac Dana Jr. died December 23rd. Havana's conquest was Britain's costliest military operation of the Seven Years War. Dr. Johnson remarked, "May my country never be cursed with such another conquest."

A little over a year before her father enlisted in Connecticut's army, Ebenezer Dana's eldest child, Mehetabel, was married in Pomfret, on December 10, 1760, to Ebenezer Allen. Her first child, Lucy, was born in Pomfret on November 24, 1762, only months after the death of Ebenezer in Havana. It is this woman, Mehetabel (Dana) Allen, who carried the "Mayflower heirloom," in old age, from Pomfret, Connecticut, to Springfield Centre, Otsego County, New York. She was eighty-six years old at the time. Her second husband, Stephen Averill—who had served in Connecticut's legislature and who, "among other farms had owned the one upon which was the famous wolf's den, which gave Gen. Israel Putnam such notoriety"—had died, and several of her children had moved to New York. Her grandson, Augustus Allen, was sixteen at the time of her arrival in New York. He writes of her in his *Brief History*: "She was small of stature, but perfect in form, and the emblem of neatness and order in her household. She had a very cheerful and amiable disposition. She was a great reader and retained all her mental faculties to the last." (Page 74)

In another place, Uncle Augustus writes of his grandmother, that she was the "daughter of Daniel Dana, of the Dana family of Massachusetts. She was born February 20, 1739, and was related to the Adams' family." (Page 65) In fact, the Pomfret records in the Barbour Collection tell us that she was born February 28, 1739, the daughter of Ebenezer Dana (Daniel Dana's son) and Mehetabel Goodell, and has no direct descents from the Adams family. But Uncle Augustus had no Barbour Collection to consult.

The Marriage of Ebenezer Allen and Mehetabel Dana

What are wonderful are the details he preserved that allow us to construct authentic pedigrees for his family. He knew there was uncertainty about the Allen pedigree; but his mentioning that his grandfather, Ebenezer Allen, had a sister, Eunice (who lived with Mehetabel (Dana) Allen even after Ebenezer's death), allows us to consult the Barbour Collection and construct the authentic Allen pedigree.

Uncle Augustus writes that his grandmother belonged to the "Dana family of Massachusetts". Not only did he not have the Barbour Collection, he also did not have Bowen's great *Genealogies of Woodstock Families*. He did not know his grandmother's father, Ebenezer, had died in Cuba; and while he was aware that numerous Dana's were early settlers in Woodstock and Pomfret, he could not place his grandmother in a pedigree and trace her relation to her Dana relatives. As an old man, no doubt he wished he had spoken with his grandmother about these things when he was a boy.

Having the pedigree of the Danas before one,[21] some interesting things are immediately noticeable. Mehetabel Dana's grandfather, Daniel, with his brothers, Jacob and Benjamin, were among the first proprietors of Pomfret. Mehetabel's great-uncle, Jacob, was married to Patience Sabine, a sister of Hannah (Sabin) Allen, the grandmother of Mehetabel's husband, Ebenezer Allen. Hanna Dana, a daughter of Jacob and Patience, marries Henry Adams, a relative of Ebenezer Allen's mother. Great Uncle Benjamin Dana has a daughter, Ann, who marries Matthew Davis Jr.—a first cousin of the Hannah Davis who is grandmother to Ebenezer Allen, while a grandson of Benjamin, Isaac Dana Jr.,

---

[21] See Chart X

was with Mehetabel's father in Cuba, dying months later from his suffering there.

Another Davis marriage[22] to a Dana—which should have amused Uncle Augustus—was the marriage of Elizabeth Davis (a sister of the China Sea captain who settled in Hawaii) to William Dana, a great-grandson of Mehetabel Dana's great-uncle, Benjamin. The child of this marriage, William Goodwin Dana, became a cabin boy on his Uncle Davis' clipper ship. His sister, Adelaide, writes to him attributing an aunt's ill health to their Uncle Capt. Davis' semi-Polynesian consort. "I think her trials," she writes, "in consequence of Uncle William's immoralities and the disgrace he has entailed upon his family have served more than anything to crush her spirits and impair her faculties. It has indeed been the means of reducing the family to a state of deep mental suffering. It was an aggravation of the blow, too, that any proofs of his infamy should thus publicly be brought forward by the transportation of his illegitimate offspring to this country."

When this letter was written in 1825, Capt. Davis had been dead for several years, but his eldest son, Robert, age five—the proof of his father's infamy—had been sent to New England to be educated. In his uncle's will, Capt. Davis left $5,000 to his nephew and cabin boy, William Goodwin Dana, who bought the brigantine *Waverly* from King Kamehameha II with it and sailed off to California where at age thirty-one, he married the sixteen year old Maria Josefa Carrillo at Mission Santa Barbara.

On hearing the news, Adelaide wrote her brother: "I was very much astonished… I congratulate you with heartfelt sincerity on any events in your life which may promote your

---

[22] See Chart III

The Marriage of Ebenezer Allen and Mehetabel Dana

happiness—though they destroy some of my own anticipations... it is painful to me to think that you are permanently locating in a foreign land..."

Adelaide married the Rev. Charles Chauncey Darling and had two children, while her brother and his wife, Maria Josefa Carrillo, had twenty-one children on their estate of some 6,000 acres south of San Luis Obispo.

Two grandsons of Mehetabel's Great Uncle, Benjamin, became ministers. The Rev. Samuel Dana graduated from Harvard in 1755 and was a minister at Groton until he was dismissed for his opposition to armed resistance against Great Britain. He then studied law and practiced in Amherst, New Hampshire, where he was buried in 1798 with Masonic honors. His daughter, Mehetabel, married the Hon. Samuel Bell, Governor of New Hampshire and United States Senator. The Rev. Joseph Dana (another of Benjamin's grandsons) was born in Pomfret and attended Yale. Numerous young men from Pomfret were at Yale at that time—a Sabine, a Chandler and a Grosvenor—and they rode down to New Haven in company on horseback. The Rev. Joseph Dana was minister at the South Church in Ipswich for sixty-two years. His daughter, Sarah, married the Hon. Israel Thorndike of Boston and was painted by Gilbert Stuart.

Much closer to Mehetabel on the Dana family tree are two first cousins, the children of her Uncle Caleb. Mehetabel was born in 1739, and Cousin George Dana in 1741. He was a sergeant in Capt. Jonathan Gate's Company of Minutemen, Col. Whitcomb's Regiment, which marched on the Lexington Alarm, April 19, 1775. His brother, James, was born in 1735 and graduated from Harvard in 1753, becoming a minister in Wallingford and New Haven during the furious struggle between the Old and New Lights. Suspected of heresy by a minority in Wallingford, the New Haven Association of Ministers attempted to block his ordination. But Wallingford had carefully picked its ordaining council and proceeded with Dana's ordination. The Association, furious, pronounced sentence of non-communion on Dana, his church and the members of the ordaining council, who in turn, broke their ties with the Association. In his book *From Puritan to Yankee*, Richard Bushman treats this struggle as an important element in the development of the American National Character. It is not, however, of any of these Danas that Uncle Augustus thought when he wrote that his grandmother belonged to "the Dana Family of Massachusetts." Only one Dana—Judge Richard Dana,[23] the founder of a distinguished line of descendents—stepped forth into the blaze of history to kindle the American Revolution with John Adams and the chief patriots of Boston. If Uncle Augustus had known that Richard Dana was the brother of his own great-grandfather—how his family piety would have thrilled! If he had known that his Grandmother Mehetabel's first cousin was the great Francis Dana, how foolish he would have felt for failing to learn from her about his exploits in the Revolution!

Uncle Augustus' great-grandfather Ebenezer Dana died in Cuba in the service of King George III on August 19, 1762. In the very next month, in Boston, the Colonies' legislature remonstrates with the Royal Governor and his Council for proposing a tax. It prays the Governor, "as he regards the peace and welfare of the province, that no measures of this nature be taken for the future," having noted that "it would be of little consequence to the people, whether they were subject to George or Louis, the

---

[23] See Chart XI

The Marriage of Ebenezer Allen and Mehetabel Dana

French King, if both were as arbitrary as both would be, if both could levy taxes without parliament..."[24]

On December 10, 1760, Mehetabel Dana married Ebenezer Allen, and her first child, Mollie, was born in November 1761. When Mollie was six months old, her grandfather, Ebenezer Dana, made out a will before going off to war for King George III. Ebenezer's daughter, Mehetabel, and her husband, Ebenezer Allen, were mentioned in this will. The following July, Ebenezer Dana arrived in Havana, and in August, he died. The next month—September, 1762—the Massachusetts' Colony's legislature declared that neither King, nor Royal Governor, nor Council may "originate" taxes. Two months later, Mehetabel (Dana) Allen's second child was born.

A rare glimpse into Mehetabel (Dana) Allen's life, between the birth of her first and second child, is given by Uncle Augustus in his *Brief History*: "In her younger days," he writes, "she used to ride from Pomfret to Boston, a distance of about eighty miles, on horseback, and take her babe with her, to visit her sister, Mrs. Bryant." (pg. 74)[25]

The road from Pomfret to Boston was part of the Middle-Boston-Post Road. As Postmaster General to the Crown, Benjamin Franklin had overseen its improvement—though no stagecoaches traveled on it until 1785. Uncle Augustus' precious glimpse of his grandmother riding horseback upon this road put her in touch with her Uncle Richard and his children in Boston at a most exciting time for the Colonies.

In the summer of 1765, (three years after Ebenezer Dana's death in the service of King George) a Boston mob hung Andrew

---

[24] Hutchinson's *History of Massachusetts Bay*, Vol. III, pg. 97
[25] A Mary Dana Bryant of Boston is mentioned in the Dana Family in America, Vol II, pg. 468, but her pedigree is not given.

Oliver in effigy. It had been reported that Oliver would be appointed Distributor of Stamps—the heinous stamps to be inflicted on the colonies by Britain's Stamp Tax Act. One night, a mob led by Ebenezer Mackintosh destroyed Oliver's house, including a looking glass said to be the largest in North America. Lieutenant Governor Hutchinson attempted to persuade the mob to disperse but was silenced by a rain of stones. The next day, August 15th, Oliver promised to do nothing to execute the Stamp Act. On August 26th, Mackintosh led his mob against Lieutenant Governor Hutchinson's house. Hutchinson writes, "They came with intoxicated rage, upon the house of the Lieutenant Governor. The doors were immediately split to pieces with broad axes, and a way made there, and at the windows, for the entry of the mob which poured in, and filled, in an instant, every room in the house."

"The Lieutenant Governor had very little notice of the approach of the mob. He directed his children, and the rest of his family, to leave the house immediately, determined to keep possession himself. His eldest daughter, after going a little way from the house returned, and refused to quit, unless her father would do the like."

"This caused him to depart from his resolution, a few minutes before the mob entered. They continued their possession until daylight; destroyed, carried away, or cast into the street, everything that was in the house; demolished every part of it, except the walls, as lay in their power; and had begun to brake away the brick work."

"The damage was estimated at twenty five hundred pounds sterling, without any regard to a great collection of public as well as private papers, in the possession and custody of the Lieutenant Governor."

"The town was, the whole night, under the awe of this mob..."[26]

The manuscript pages of the second volume of Hutchinson's *History* were scattered abroad in that rainy night—and saved by the solicitude of a neighbor, before more than a few pages were rendered unintelligible.

Months passed and Andrew Oliver, who was Secretary of the Colony, went unmolested after resigning his place as Stamp Distributor. But on December 16th, he received an anonymous letter directing him "to appear the next day, under the *liberty* tree, to make a public resignation, and to acquaint him, that his non-compliance would bring on him the displeasure of the 'true-born son's of liberty...'"

The Secretary (Oliver) being informed that the people were assembled (at the liberty tree) before the time, by a note directed to them, desired to make his resignation at the townhouse, but this would not satisfy them, and they insisted on his coming to the tree! Several of his friends, at his desire, accompanied him; but Mackintosh, the chief-actor in destroying the Lieutenant Governor's house, attended him, at his right hand, through the streets to the tree, in a rainy tempestuous day, a great number following. About two thousand people were assembled. Several of the selectmen, and many other persons of condition, were in the house before which the tree stood; with RICHARD DANA Esq., a justice of the peace and a lawyer of note, who administered an oath to the secretary..."

Concerning Dana's action, Hutchinson writes, "This indignity to the third crown officer in rank in the province passed without notice from any authority... In regular times, the

---

[26] Hutchinson's *History of Massachusetts Bay*, Vol. III, pg. 124

governor and council would have immediately dismissed the justice of the peace from his office; but it passed now, as if he had been in the regular execution of it. Some imagined that it would provoke Parliament to show its resentment, while others, who made a better conjecture, expected that it would promote the repeal of the Act."[27]

The riots of the Boston Mob during the Stamp Act crisis caused the British to send their army into Boston. But the British soldiers soon came to feel that the judicial system they were charged to strengthen had it in for them. In October 1669, the British Guard at Boston Neck was attacked. Judge Richard Dana addresses several British soldiers in the preliminary hearing in these terms: "Who brought you here? Who sent for you? By what authority do you mount guard, or march in the streets with arms? It is contrary to the laws of the Province, and you should be taken up for so offending. We want none of your guards. We have arms of our own and can protect ourselves. You are but a handful. Better take care not to provoke us. If you do, you must take the consequences." This tension between the soldiers and provincials led to the Boston Massacre, after which Judge Dana sent Captain Preston to jail for having ordered the British soldiers to fire on the crowd.

Edmund Trowbridge, Judge Dana's brother-in-law, was the Colony's Attorney General, and as such, feared an attack by the mob on his house and family or a visit from the Sons of Liberty—the power (including his brother-in-law, Judge Dana) behind the mob. In these circumstances, Trowbridge—possessing a portrait of Lieutenant Governor Hutchinson—thought it prudent to take this portrait from its frame, to burn it, and

---

[27] Hutchinson's *History*, Vol III, pg. 140

to replace it with Copley's portrait of his brother-in-law, Judge Richard Dana. Had ten or twenty of Copley's portraits of the merchants and lawyers of Boston been known to the members of Britain's Parliament, perhaps they would have hesitated before taxing them.

Judge Dana presided at a meeting in Commemoration of the Boston Massacre, held in 1772 in Faneuil Hall, only two months before his death. John Adams spoke of Judge Dana as "One who, had he not been cut off by death, would have furnished one of the immortal names of the Revolution."

The *Dictionary of American Biography* states that Dana's death was regarded as "a severe if not irreparable loss to the Colonial cause." It sketches his character: "Of unimpeachable integrity, unswerving principles, and a fanatic in his devotion to duty as he saw it, his was a strong and impressive but unattractive personality. Austere to the point of parsimony." These are the words from the *Boston Gazette,* June 1, 1772: Judge Dana "was exemplary in Carefulness, Diligence, and Frugality, whereby he has left to his widow… and to his children… a handsome fortune… A very steady and strenuous, and it must be confessed, many times a passionate opposer of all those… who in his judgment were enemies to the Civil and Religious Rights of his Country; and he very well understood what those rights were."

Among the children of Judge Dana (the first cousins of Mehetabel [Dana] Allen) one, Edmund Dana, went to England, became an Anglican clergyman, and married a daughter of the sixth Baron Kinnard. Another, Francis Dana, was graduating from Harvard at the time Mehetabel was riding from Pomfret to Boston with her babe.

"In 1779 when John Adams was appointed minister plenipotentiary to negotiate peace with England, Francis Dana was sent

Ancestor Worship

Portrait of Judge Richard Dana 1699–1772 by John Singleton Copley
Courtesy National Park Service, Longfellow National Historic Site

The Marriage of Ebenezer Allen and Mehetabel Dana

to France with him as secretary of the legation. The two men, who had formerly been associated in their legal work in Boston, reached Paris in February 1780. Finding little opportunity there even to talk peace, Adams went to Holland for the purpose of negotiating a loan, and if possible a treaty. In June, Congress sent Dana a supplementary commission, authorizing him, in the event of the possible disability of Adams, to continue negotiating for loans." Later, "Congress determined to send a regularly accredited minister to Catherine of Russia, and chose Dana for this diplomatic venture... Before setting out for St. Petersburg, Dana consulted his American friends in Europe, particularly John Adams, whose youthful son, John Quincy, whom he took with him to Russia as secretary... Dana was one of the few leaders of the day looked upon with real affection by John and John Quincy Adams." *(Dictionary of American Biography)* He died in 1811, at the age of seventy-eight, while his cousin, Mehetabel (Dana) Allen lived another eighteen years and died in 1829 at eighty-nine years of age.

Our own families' knowledge of the closeness of this relationship between Francis Dana and the Adams' Presidents seems to have penetrated even to Mehetabel (Dana) Allen's grandson, Augustus Allen, for in his *Brief History*, he states, quite wrongly, that John Quincy Adams was descended from the Dana's.

In closing, we must remark on two of Francis Dana's sons (the second cousins of our ancestor, Mehetabel's son, Nathan Allen). Richard Henry Dana I began his public life with his expulsion from Harvard for his part in the Rotten Cabbage Rebellion of 1807, and persevered in his revolutionary course to the end. In the controversy between the Trinitarians and the Unitarians, he sided with the Trinitarians and, in later life, became an Episcopalian. He gave up a political life for a literary life and

Ancestor Worship

Three generations of Richard Henry Danas

Courtesy National Park Service, Longfellow National Historic Site

was one of the founding editors of the *North American Review*; but he championed Wordsworth and Coleridge before they were popular and "said that Pope was not a poet at all, which was too much for his friends and much too much for Boston. A furious hubbub resounded through the town. Out Dana went, and out went with him any hope that the *North American Review* would ever understand the new generation."[28]

His burial in the old burying ground in Cambridge is described in Longfellow's *The Burial of the Poet*:

> In the old churchyard of his
> native town,
> And in the ancestral tomb
> beside the wall,
> We laid him in the sleep that
> comes to all,
> And left him to his rest and
> his renown.
>
> The snow was falling...

His son, Richard Henry Dana Jr., was in Thoreau's class at Harvard, and wrote *Two Years Before the Mast*, in which he deplores the Yankee sea captains who "leave their conscience at the horn" to become Catholics and marry California senoritas—failing to mention that his cousin, William Goodwin Dana, was one of these.

Two Years Before the Mast included a description of a coastal headland which would later be called Dana Point.

---

[28] *The Flowering of New England*, Van Wyck Brooks, pg. 119.

Of the children of Francis Dana Jr., Sophia (Dana) Ripley should be mentioned. She was a third cousin to Mehetabel (Dana) Allen's grandson, Nathan Prescott Allen; and the wife of the Unitarian minister, Rev. George Ripley. After fourteen years preaching in a Boston pulpit, Ripley resigned. He and Sophia were already living at the farm nine miles out of Boston at West Roxbury, which was to become Brook Farm, the paragon of Utopian Communes. The first meeting of the "Transcendental Club" had taken place at the Ripley's house in Boston, and he was a founder of its magazine, the *Dial*. Emerson and Alcott were visitors at Brook Farm, while Hawthorne had invested in it and worked there as a laborer. Ripley, the Archon, was up before dawn, milking, cleaning the stalls, carting vegetables off to market or preparing his Sunday lecture on Kant or Spinoza. There were merry dances every night, picnics on Cow Island or in the grove, boating parties on the Charles, Elizabethan pageants and charades. Like her husband, Sophia worked ten hours a day—much to the annoyance of her family—in the muslin room, washing, scrubbing the floors, and nursing a Philipino leper, Lucas Corales. While her husband taught philosophy and mathematics, she taught history and a Dante class in Italian. Her distant cousin, Charles A. Dana, taught Greek and German.

In New York, Horace Greeley's newspaper, the *Tribune*, was promoting the ideas of the socialist Fourier. The members at Brook Farm adopted Fourier's ideas, and turned themselves into a "phalanestery." After the collapse of the farm that followed, George Ripley and Charles A. Dana found work writing for the *Tribune*. During this time, George and Sophia (Dana) Ripley lived in a single room, in a shabby boarding house in a dingy street in Brooklyn, New York. While George wrote his elegant, scholarly essays on Lessing and Voltaire and Spencer for the *Tribune*, Sophia dedicated herself to caring for poor children on Randolph's Island and New York City's prostitutes. She had become a Roman Catholic—converted by the convert, Father Hecker, who had been with her at Brook Farm. He published her translation of St. Catherine of Genoa's *Vita e Dottrina*. She was a principal patroness of the Sisters of the Good Shepherd, working tirelessly to establish them in New York with the grudging consent of Bishop Hughes.

In their dingy boarding house, in that single room, Sophia (Dana) Ripley died of cancer in 1861. Her husband lived another twenty years, during which he worked with Charles A. Dana on *The New American Encyclopedia*. It brought him money and travel and a handsome carriage to drive about in Central Park. When he came to die—though not a Catholic—he called for Father Hecker; but when Father Hecker came, it was too late.

CHART I:
Some Allen Cousins

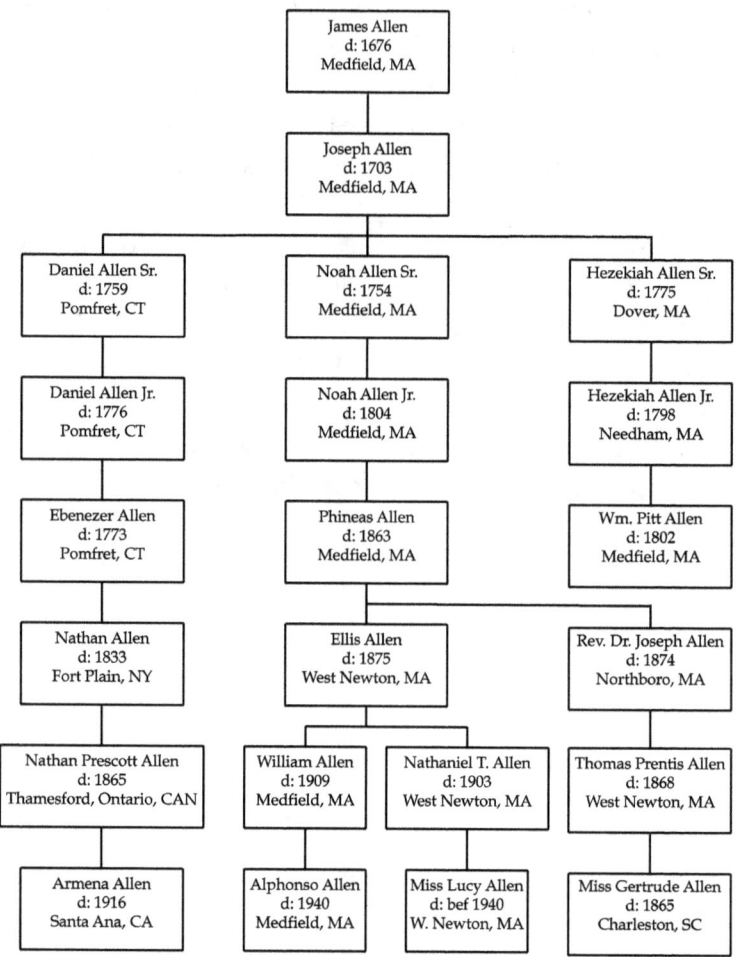

The Marriage of Ebenezer Allen and Mehetabel Dana

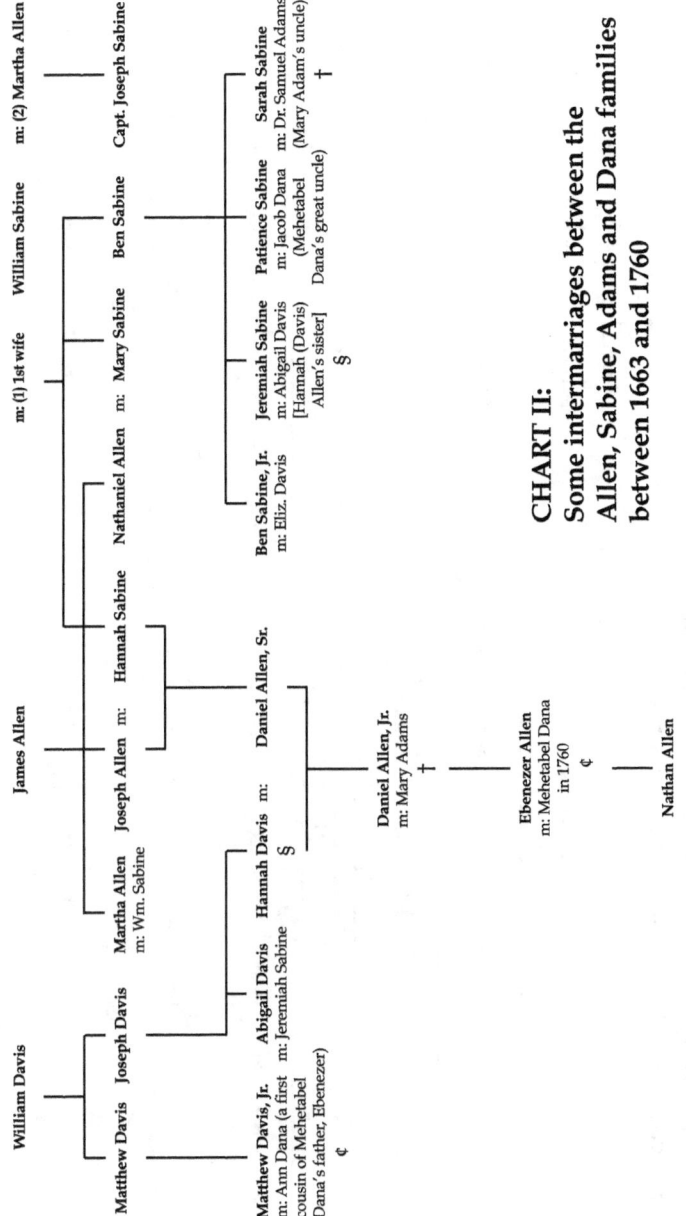

CHART II:
Some intermarriages between the Allen, Sabine, Adams and Dana families between 1663 and 1760

Chart III:
Illustrating the author's double relationship with California's Estudillo and Carrillo Families by way of his Dana and Davis ancestresses

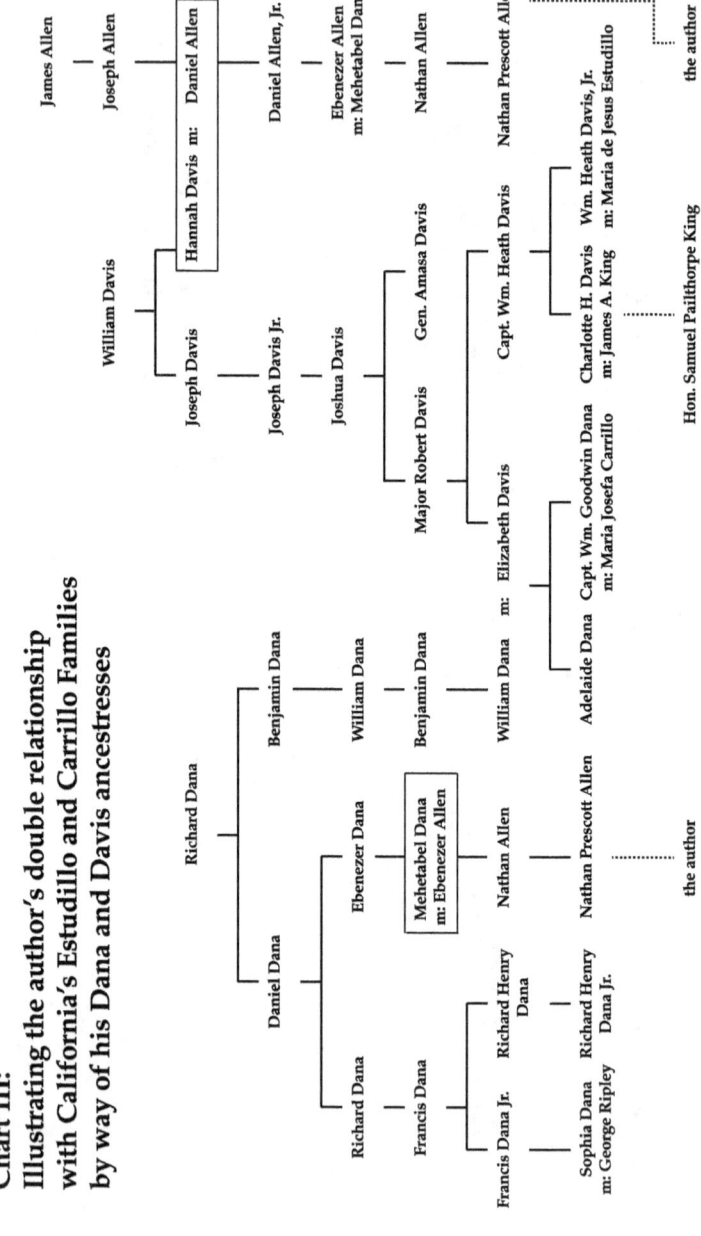

The Marriage of Ebenezer Allen and Mehetabel Dana

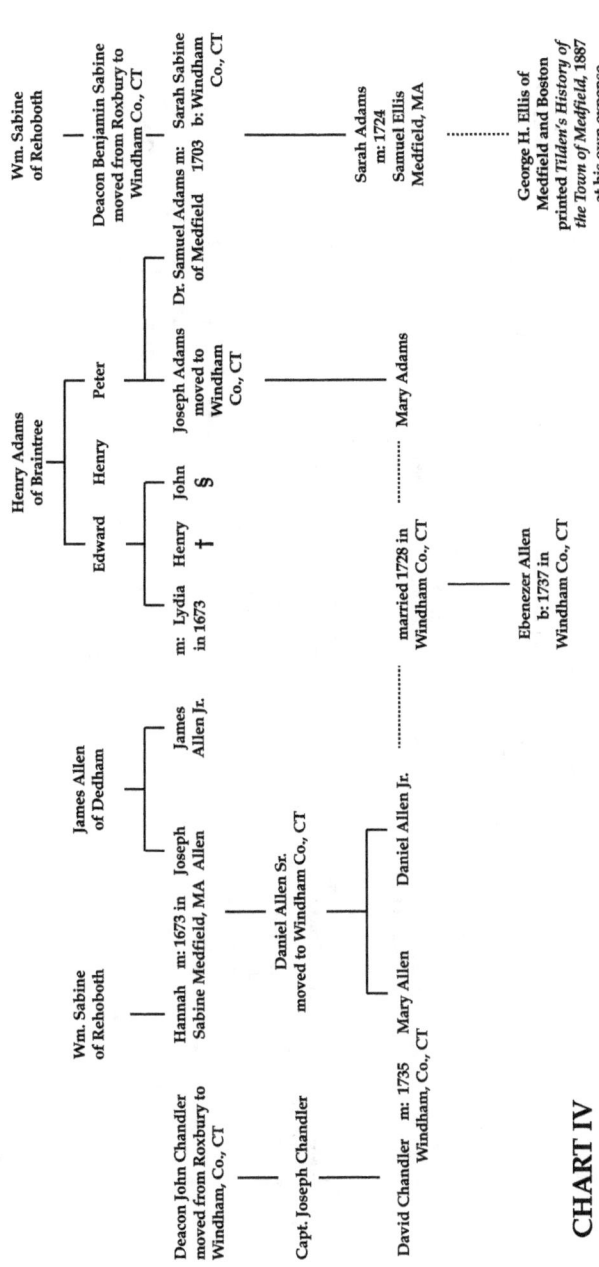

CHART IV

† Henry Adams married Hannah Dana, daughter of Patience Sabine and Jacob Dana, first cousin of Ebenezer Dana, 1711–1762
§ Ancestor of King Leka of Albania

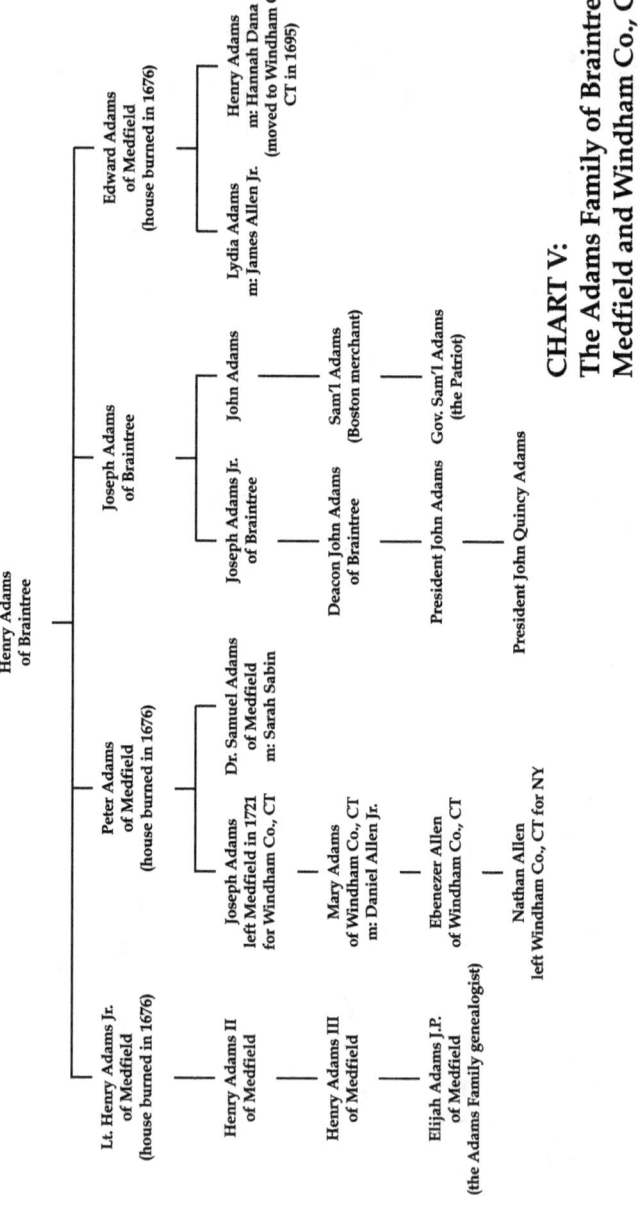

CHART V:
The Adams Family of Braintree, Medfield and Windham Co., CT

The Marriage of Ebenezer Allen and Mehetabel Dana

CHART VI: The Chandlers and their matrimonial alliance with the Allens and Mehetabel's uncle, Caleb Dana

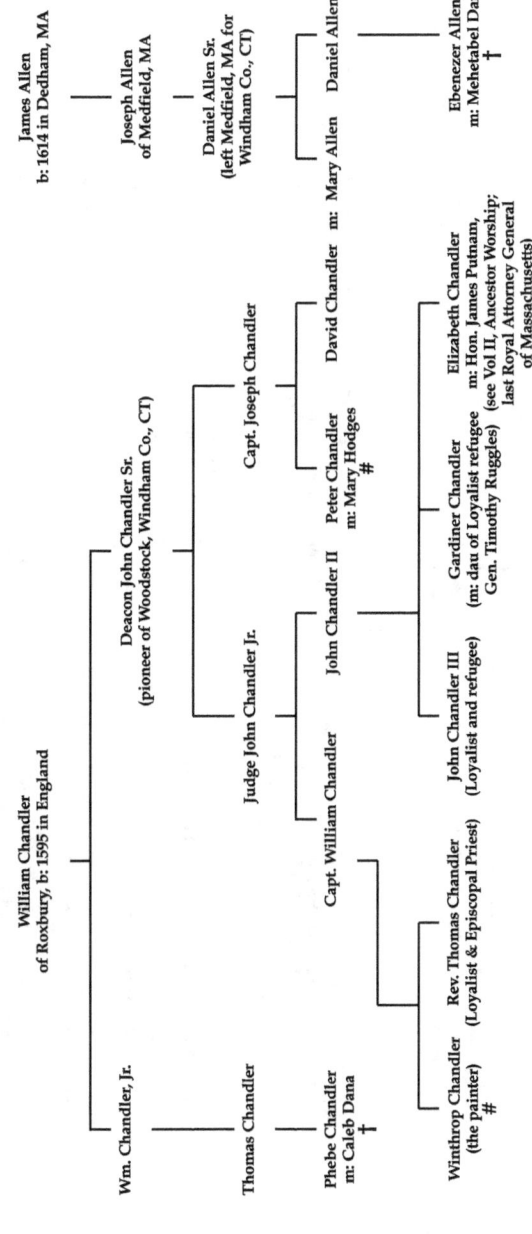

† Caleb Dana is Mehetabel Dana's uncle; he grew rich as a quartermaster in the French & Indian War.

Mary (Hodges) Chandler was painted by Winthrop Chandler; her great-grandson, Herbert W. Bowen, was the stupendous genealogist and historian of Woodstock, Windham Co., CT.

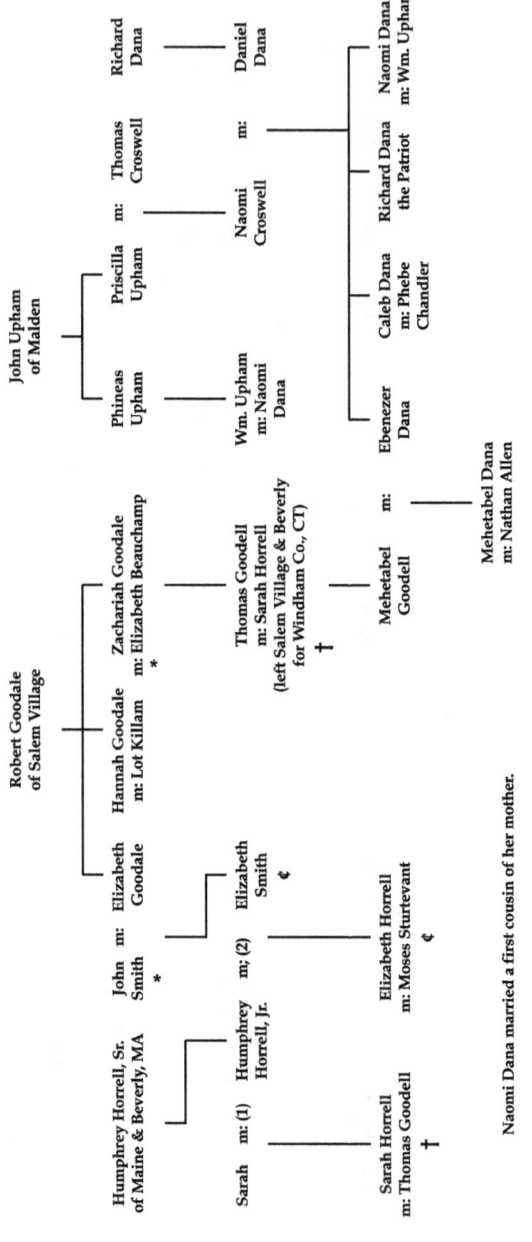

The Marriage of Ebenezer Allen and Mehetabel Dana

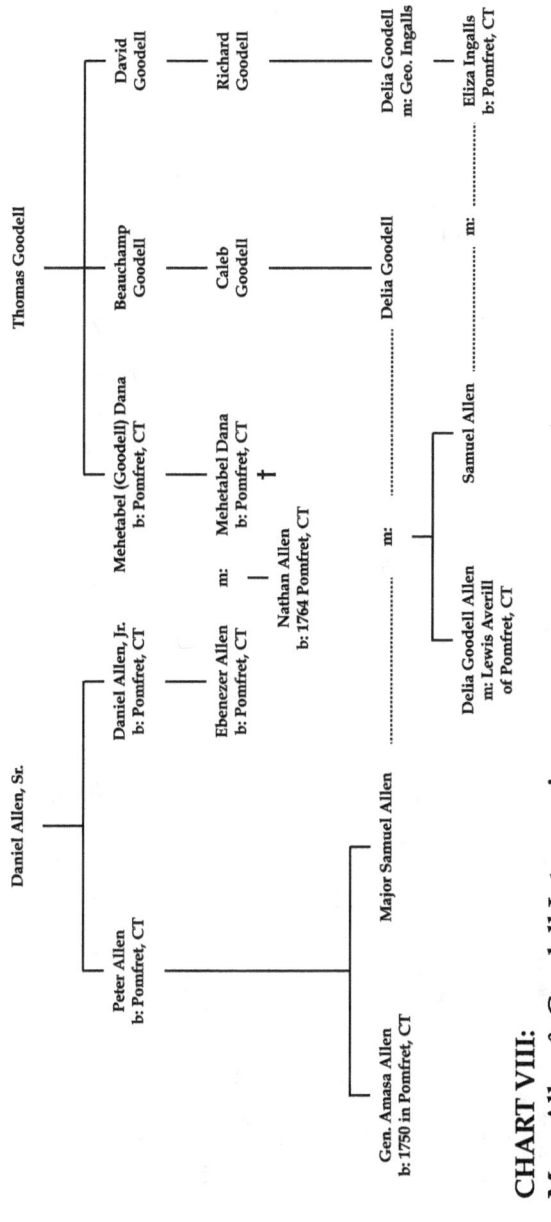

CHART VIII:
More Allen & Goodell Intermarriages

† Mehetabel (Dana) Allen married secondly Hon. Stephen Averill, no doubt an ancestor of Lewis Averill.

Brig. General Amasa Allen, first cousin of Nathan Allen, was at Dorchester Heights in the Revolutionary War at the time of the evacuation, and worked through the night of March 4, 1776, with Rufus Putnam, to fortify the place. He went to Walpole, NH, a poor man and became a State Senator and proprietor of the journal *Political Observatory*. His military funeral in Wolpole was the largest ever known in that place. Cousin Herbert Bowen's "Genealogies of Woodstock Families" states that the General's portrait was "exhibited at the Antique Art and Loan Exhibition in Putnam, March 15-20, 1880, catalogue nos. 970-71", and that "his coat of arms now belongs to his niece, Mrs. Delia Goodell (Allen) Averill of Pomfret." Is this the coat of arms recorded by Augustus Allen in his *"Brief History"*?

Ancestor Worship

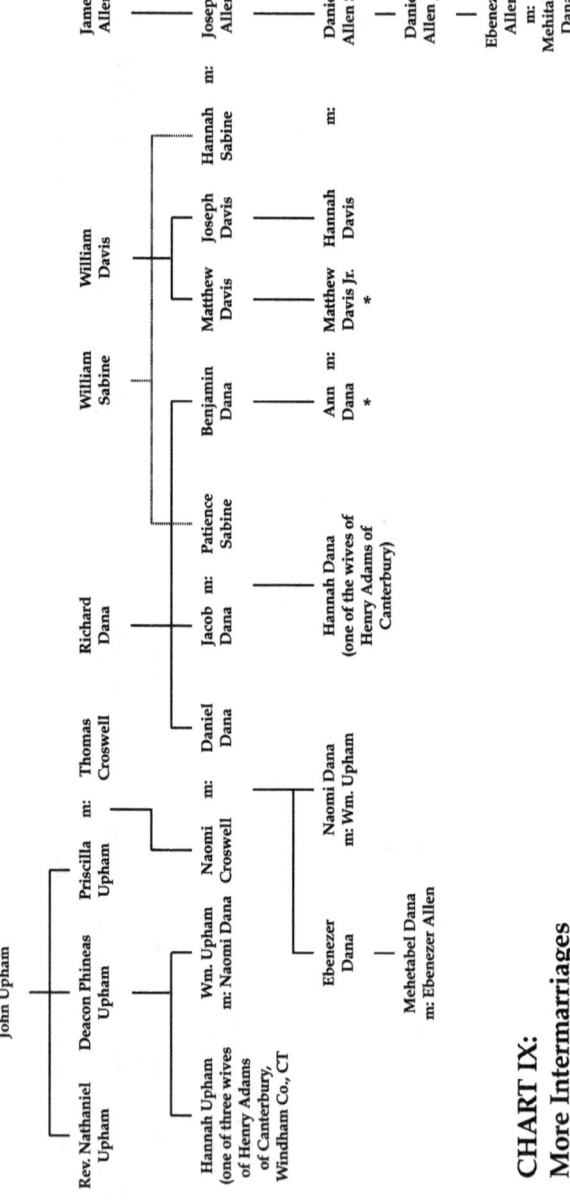

**CHART IX:
More Intermarriages**

* Mehetabel (Dana) Allen's father's cousin, Ann Dana, married Mehetabel's husband Ebenezer Allen's mother's cousin, Matthew Davis, Jr.

Mehetabel (Dana) Allen's aunt, Naomi Dana, married Mehetabel's great-grandmother Priscilla (Upham) Croswell's nephew, William Upham.

Wives of Henry Adams of Canterbury, Windham Co., CT

The Marriage of Ebenezer Allen and Mehetabel Dana

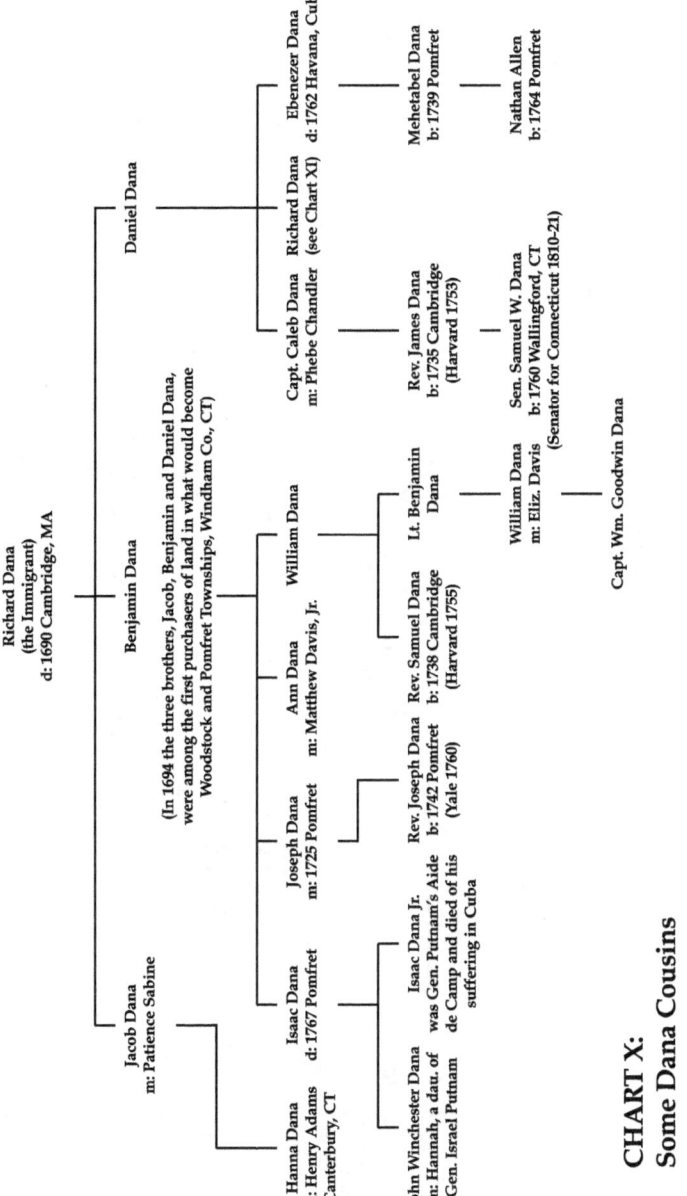

**CHART X:
Some Dana Cousins**

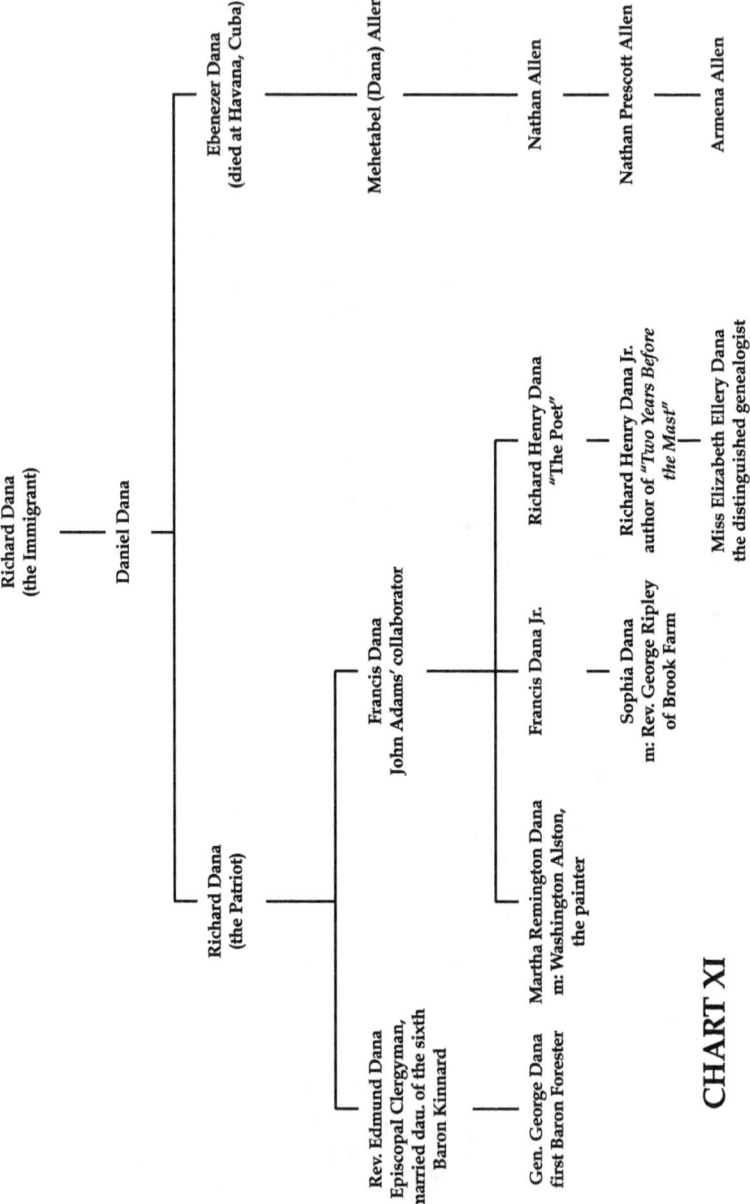

CHART XI

Bibliography

Augustus Allen, *A Brief History of the Family of Nathan Allen,* Poughkeepsie, NY, 1895

Lucy Allen, *Memorial of Joseph and Lucy Clark Allen,* George H. Ellis, printer, Boston, 1891

Joseph Allen, *History of the Worcester Association,* Boston, 1868

Richard Bushman, *From Puritan to Yankee,* Harvard, 1967

Thomas Church, *The History of Philip's War,* J. & B. Williams, Exeter, NH, 1843

Thomas Hutchinson, *History of Massachusetts Bay Colony,* 1764–1828

Ellen Larned, *History of Windham County, Connecticut,* 1874

Douglas Leach, *Flintlock and Tomahawk,* Norton Library, 1966

Jill Lepore, *The Name of War*, Vintage Books, 1999

Kenneth Lockridge, *A New England Town, The First One Hundred Years*, Norton & Co., 1970

William Tilden, *History of the Town of Medfield, Mass., 1650–1886 with Genealogies of the Families*, Geo. Ellis, publisher, Boston, 1887

Name Index

Adams Jr., Peter (b: 1653), 49
Adams, Dr. Samuel (b: 1670), 44, 46
Adams, Henry (b: 1582), 44–45, 47–48, 75
Adams, Henry (b: 1663), 53
Adams, John (b: 1691), 44–45, 46–47, 78, 83, 85
Adams, John Quincy (b: 1767), 12, 46–47, 85
Adams, Joseph (b: 1654), 44–45
Adams, Joseph (b: 1668), 49
Adams, Mary (b: 1705), 43, 45, 48–49
Adams, Peter (b: 1622), 45, 48–49
Allen, Abigail (b: 1694), 3
Allen, Armena (b: 1841), ii, ix, xix, xxi–xxiii, 1–3, 31, 50, 90
Allen, Augustus Lovanzo (b: 1809), xxiii–xxiv, 1, 13–15, 45, 47, 60, 68–72, 74–76, 78–79, 85, 101
Allen, Capt. Sabine, 4
Allen, Daniel Jr. (b: 1706), 43, 45, 49–51, 53, 90–92
Allen, Daniel Sr. (b: 1681), 2–3, 31–33, 37–38, 90–92
Allen, David (b: 1683), 2, 37, 43
Allen, Ebenezer (b: 1737), ix, 51, 53–54, 73–75, 79, 90–92
Allen, Eleazer (b: 1688), 2
Allen, Ellis (b: 1792), 5, 7–8, 90
Allen, Hannah (b: 1679), 2
Allen, Hezekiah (b: 1692), 3, 90
Allen, Horatio Philanzo (b: 1809), xxii–xxiii
Allen, James (b: 1614), 1–2, 13, 15, 17–21, 26, 31, 90–92
Allen, James Jr. (b: 1646), 26, 45
Allen, Jeremiah (b: 1690), 2

Allen, Joseph H. (b: 1820), 12
Allen, Joseph Jr. (b: 1676), 2, 38
Allen, Joseph Sr. (b: 1654), 2–3, 5–6, 9, 19, 22, 26, 31, 91
Allen, Lucy (b: 1867), 2, 90, 101
Allen, Martha (b: 1641), 21–23, 26–27, 32, 36, 91
Allen, Mary (b: 1715), 50
Allen, Nathan Prescott (b: 1793), 88, 90, 92
Allen, Nathaniel (b: 1648), 22
Allen, Nathaniel Topliff (b: 1823), 7, 90
Allen, Nehemiah (b: 1699), 3
Allen, Noah (b: 1685), 3, 90
Allen, Noah Jr. (b: 1719), 3–4, 11
Allen, Phineas (b: 1692), 4–5, 9–11
Allen, Phineas Jr. (b: 1801), 10, 90
Allen, Prescott (b: 1836), xxi, 10
Allen, Rev. Joseph (Phineas) (b: 1790), 6, 8, 12
Allen, William (b: 1830), 12, 90
Allen, William Pitt (b: 1766), 3, 90
Averill, Stephen (b: 1730), 74

Beauchamp, Elizabeth (b: 1648), 64–66

Bulkeley, Rev. Peter (b: 1641), xxiii, xxiv
Bullard, Ann (b: 1626), 55

Chamberlain, Edmund (b: 1617), 38
Chandler, Capt. Joseph (b: 1683), 50, 53
Chandler, David (b: 1712), 50
Chandler, Deacon John (b: 1634), 50, 59–60
Chandler, Winthrop (b: 1747), 50–51
Croswell, Naomi (b: 1670), 56, 58
Crosswell, Thomas (b: 1633), 58

Dana Jr., Francis (b: 1777), 88
Dana, Ann (b: 1705), 53, 75
Dana, Benjamin (b: 1660), 50, 53, 59, 75
Dana, Caleb (b: 1697), 77
Dana, Daniel (b: 1663), 50, 53, 58, 75
Dana, Ebenezer (b: 1711), 59, 72–75, 78–79
Dana, Francis (b: 1743), 78, 83, 85
Dana, Jacob (b: 1654), 50, 53, 59, 75
Dana, Judge Richard (b: 1699), 78, 81–84

Name Index

Dana, Mehetabel (b: 1739), ix, 51, 53–54, 70–71, 73–79, 83, 85, 88
Dana, Rev. Joseph (b: 1742), 77
Dana, Rev. Samuel (b: 1739), 77
Dana, Richard (b: 1617), 54, 78–79
Dana, Richard Henry Jr. (b: 1815), 87
Dana, Richard Henry Sr. (b: 1787), 85–86
Dana, Robert (b: 1571), 54
Dana, Samuel (b: 1694), 44
Dana, William (b: 1767), 76, 87
Dana, William Goodwin (b: 1800), 33, 39
Davis Jr., Joseph (b: 1673), 38–40
Davis Jr., Matthew (b: 1706), 54, 75
Davis Jr., William Heath (b: 1822), 39
Davis, Capt. William Heath (b: 1796), 39–41, 76
Davis, Elizabeth (b: 1778), 76
Davis, Hanna (b: 1685), 53, 75
Davis, Hannah (b: 1680), 33, 35–36, 38–41, 54, 75
Davis, Jonathan (b: 1665), 35
Davis, Matthew (b: 1664), 33–34, 36, 39

Estudillo, Maria de Jesus (b: 1829), 39
Everett, Edward, 5–8, 10

Garrison, William Lloyd, 8
Gay, Sarah (b: 1692), 3–4
Goodale, Jacob (b: 1642), 66, 68
Goodale, Robert (b: 1601), 63–64
Goodell, Mehetabel (b: 1717), 59–60, 70–74
Goodell, Thomas (b: 1676), 59–60 63–64, 68–69, 71–72
Guild, Anna (b: 1638), 2, 17, 19, 21

Holmes, Hannah (b: 1800), 39
Horrell Jr., Humphrey (b: 1650), 61–63
Horrell, Sarah (b: 1684), 59–60, 63–64, 68, 71–72

King, Samuel Pailthorpe (b: 1916), 39–40

Mann, Horace, 7, 11–12
Massasoit, 22–23
McLellan, Charlotte Gertrude (b: 1893), xviii, xix, xxi
McLellan, John (b: 1836), xx
McLellan, Nathan John Frederick (Fred) (b: 1865), xx

Newcombe, Rachel (b: 1631), 48

Philip (King), 23, 24, 29, 61
Prentiss, Thomas, 5

Sabin, Benjamin (b: 1646), 24, 31–37, 43, 50, 53
Sabin, Experience (b: 1648), 44
Sabin, Hannah (b: 1654), 2, 22, 26–27, 32, 36–38, 43–45, 53, 75
Sabin, Jeremiah (b: 1657), 24, 38
Sabin, John (b: 1666), 50, 53
Sabin, Joseph (b: 1645), 23
Sabin, Nehemiah (b: 1647), 27, 32
Sabin, Patience (b: 1655), 53, 75

Sabin, Samuel (b: 1640), 25, 35
Sabin, William (b: 1609), 21–23, 27–28, 36
Sabine, Daniel (b: 1676), 37
Sabine, Experience (b: 1685), 44
Sabine, Mary (b: 1652), 22
Sabine, Nehemiah (b: 1680), 37, 44
Sabine, Sarah (b: 1679), 44
Sabine, Stephen (b: 1689), 44

Upham, John (b: 1597), 56–58
Upham, Priscilla (b: 1642), 57

Ware, Lucy, 6
Winslow, Josiah (b: 1606), 24–25